València

TRIANGLE ▼ BOOKS

Essential Valencia
Text **Jaime Millás**

Essential
Valencia

Main Fallera and her cortège (Fallera Major i Cort d'Honor)

Contents

Ciutat Vella page 08 | **La Seu** page 11 | **La Xerea** page 24 | **El Carme** page 32 | **El Mercat** page 42 | **Sant Francesc** page 50 | **Velluters** page 57 | **L'Eixample** page 58 | **Valencian** *Modernisme* page 61 | **Russafa** page 67 | **Túria Gardens** page 70 | **City of Arts and Sciences** page 82 | **The Port, El Cabanyal and the Beaches** page 90 | **City of the Future** page 100 | **L'Albufera and L'Horta** page 106 | **Festivities, Traditions and Gastronomy** page 116 | **And also...** page 126 |

Annex **Thematic Routes**

Valencia, a Mediterranean city

with a cultural and social history dating back 2000 years, has a first-rate artistic and natural heritage. Valencia is Gothic, Baroque, *Modernista* (Valencian Art Nouveau) and contemporary. It was also a Moorish city, though little remains from that period. The Romans and Visigoths left significant traces, however. The Iberians as well, in the nearest mountains.

A city open to the sea, it was the leader of Mediterranean trade in the 15th century, and also headed the political and cultural activity of the Crown of Aragon. The destiny of the Vatican was in the hands of the Valencian Borgias (Callixtus III and Alexander VI) at the time.

The Silk Exchange (Llotja de la Seda) is the Gothic icon of this geopolitical hegemony and one of the world's architectural marvels, declared a UNESCO World Heritage Site. The splendour of the period is reflected in the monumentality of the cathedral, the Holy Grail it keeps within its sturdy walls, and the stupendous Gothic retables hanging in the halls of the Fine Arts Museum.

All architectural styles are present in Valencia, because it

Silk Exchange (Llotja de la Seda)

Valencia, a Mediterranean City

has always been a receptor of cultures through its maritime and land routes, both inland and coastal. It is located at kilometre 9,090 of the Silk Route. Each year at the Falles celebrations, the silk dresses of the *falleres* (the women participating in the festival) evoke an industrial tradition that has been essential to the city.

The southern lifestyle is patent in its streets, beaches and restaurants, at marketplaces and squares. A cosmopolitan atmosphere is marked by the thousands of visitors who admire the old and are dazzled by the monumental new architecture and urban design. Valencia is truly a pleasure to the eye. It is full of nuances and contrasts.

The city boasts a large historic centre in which Baroque buildings form part of its identity. The Cathedral's Portal of the Irons (Porta dels Ferros), distinguished by the influence of Bernini, the church at the Monastery of Sant Miquel dels Reis, the Church of Saints John (Església del Sant Joan del Mercat) across from the Silk Exchange, the Church of Saint Nicholas (Sant Nicolau), and many other churches and palaces in the city illustrate the enthusiasm with which Valencian architects

The Cathedral's Portal of the Irons

and artists made the Baroque theirs. In many cases, they also successfully combined Gothic or other medieval structures with a new ornamental architectural skin in the Baroque spirit.

At the turn of the 20th century, Valencia experienced another of its historical stages of profound change. The economic boom generated by the citrus trade and the industrialisation of artisan sectors contributed to urban transformation. The city walls that protected the Old City since Moorish times were torn down and new urban districts were built with magnificent examples of *Modernista* and Neogothic architecture. Francesc Mora became the architect in fashion. With his imagination and technical know-how, he designed the North Station, the Exposition Palace, Columbus Market Hall and an extensive inventory of housing for the upper middle class, as well as reforming the City Hall.

After a tragic flood in the mid-20th century, the municipal government decided to reroute the River Túria to go around the city and, through pressure from citizens and professional organisations, turned the riverbed into an immense garden

Clock at North Station (Estació del Nord)

Valencia, a Mediterranean City

for leisure and sports. The City of Arts and Sciences cultural complex built there has become an icon of the contemporary city's modernity and innovation, only one of the new uses to which the riverbed-turned-gardens has been put.

As the political capital of the Autonomous Community of Valencia, the city hosts its institutions of self-government approved in 1982. It is an officially bilingual society. Hence, street signs and shops are often in both Spanish and Valencian. The third-largest capital city in Spain in population (circa 800,000), Valencia receives some 1,800,000 visitors a year.

It is one of the most beloved tourist destinations in Spain.

Its visitors particularly enjoy the cultural offer of its 47 museums and the sunny beaches of its dune, pine grove and sand coastline. They appreciate its abundance of nature, and the tradition of its gardens and orange groves. Because if its maritime, Mediterranean nature, its population enjoys life outside the home. There are excellent weather conditions (average temperature of 19.2 °C / 66.6 °F) for spending time outdoors. It's a city of many options for those who choose to make it their own, if only for a few days.

City of Arts and Sciences

Ciutat Vella
The heart of the city

Valencia a vista de pájaro (Bird's-eye View of Valencia, 1858), engraving by A. Guesdon, L. Giménez Lorente Collection, Huguet Archives.

Ciutat Vella

At the centre of the historic area, Ciutat Vella (the Old City) is divided into six neighbourhoods: La Seu, La Xerea, El Carme, El Mercat, Sant Francesc and El Pilar (also known as Velluters, i.e. Velvet-Makers). The perimeter of the former city walls built by the Christian kings marks the border with the modern area of the expansion district (*eixample*) built when the walls were torn down. In the Old City, you can still see remains of the Moorish wall, smaller in circumference. Over time, two focal points arose: a more select area represented by the Church and the municipal institutions, and another area with the marketplace and artisans.

Ciutat Vella | La Seu

La Seu

The historic kernel of the city, this neighbourhood is organised around the magnificent building of La Seu (the cathedral). The Romans chose this area to build Valentia. The Visigoths strengthened its importance, as did the Moors. In the Christian period, the neighbourhood consolidated its function as the heart of the city.

The institutions of Valencia's civil and religious powers have their headquarters here. Visiting this area thus allows you to take in the most beautiful buildings and experience the city's main customs and cultural traditions.

It is bordered by the Túria Gardens, Carrer de la Pau, Carrer de les Avellanes and Carrer dels Serrans. Its perimeter follows the outlines of a former island in the river. Its streets are at a slightly higher elevation than the remainder of Ciutat Vella. The only reminder of its Moorish past is the layout of its streets and the ruins of the Great Mosque and the Alcàsser or palace, buried under the cathedral and the Archbishop's Palace, respectively.

El Micalet

The tallest bell tower in medieval Valencia, El Micalet was built by Andreu Julià in the style typical for churches in Catalonia and Languedoc at the time. Its 207-step spiral staircase leads to a terrace 51 metres above street level. At its tallest point, the tower measures nearly 60 metres. For centuries, it was the best viewpoint over the city, the surrounding gardens and the sea. Its twelve bells have been ringing on feast days since the 15th century.

El Tribunal de les Aigües

Each Thursday, the Water Tribunal convenes at the Cathedral's Portal of the Apostles to settle conflicts over the distribution of irrigation water supplied by a network of irrigation channels developed by the Moors. This tribunal, declared UNESCO Intangible World Heritage, has been administering justice for a thousand years.

Carrer del Micalet

← **El Micalet bell tower**

Water Tribunal (Tribunal de les Aigües)

↑ Santa Caterina's Gothic façade on Lope de Vega Square   ↓ Orxateria de Santa Catalina (tiger nut parlour)

Ciutat Vella | La Seu

Santa Caterina
(Saint Catherine's Church)

This mosque-turned-Gothic-temple was consecrated after the Christian reconquest by King James I of the Crown of Aragon. Its baroque tower, the work of Joan Baptista Vinyes, was built between 1686 and 1704. Its hexagonal floor plan recalls the lines of the monumental Micalet tower. The bells were cast in London in 1729 and in 1914, a clock was added but recently removed as part of a restoration project that would return the bell formerly hanging there to its place.

In the late 19th century, Carrer de la Pau was opened up, leading right up to the bell tower. This reform significantly improved connections of the Old City with the inner ring road and the sea. It also created one of the most beautiful perspectives of the historic city centre: Santa Caterina's baroque bell tower was in the symmetrical centre at one end of the modern street.

Santa Caterina, Gothic nave

Orxateries or horchaterías
(Tiger Nut Parlours)

Near Santa Caterina church is the eponymous Horchatería, an emblematic tiger nut parlour serving *orxata* / *horchata* (tiger nut milk) with *fartons* (sweet buns), *llet gelada* / *leche merengada* (sugared milk with cinnamon and lemon rind), and Valencian ultra-thick hot chocolate with *bunyols* (fritters), at traditional marble-top tables with ironwork legs. *Orxata* is a sweet refreshment made of *xufes* or tiger nuts (*Cyperus esculentus*) from the gardens of nearby Alboraia.

Santa Caterina's Baroque bell tower

↑ El Micalet and the Baroque Portal of the Irons façade at Plaça de la Reina   ↓ The Gothic Portal of the Apostles

La Seu
(The Cathedral)

Started in 1262 over the ruins of a former mosque, construction continued until the mid-18th century, which was when the Gothic parts were concealed. Fortunately, today it has recovered its former aspect. It is the city's most important religious building. It has a nave and two side aisles, and a polygonal apse topped by a two-storey octagonal lantern tower with sixteen windows on its two levels. The works were begun by Master Arnau Vidal according to early Gothic design. They concluded in 1702, in the Baroque period, with the intervention of Konrad Rudolf and Francesc Vergara.

This potpourri of styles can be seen in the three portals: the Palau or Palace Portal is in an archaic Romanesque fused with early Gothic; the Apostles' Portal in pure Gothic; and the Portal of the Irons (Portada dels Ferros), in Baroque. The latter evokes the Roman style of the brilliant sculptor Bernini.

A visit to the Chapel of the Holy Grail is a must. The relic of the Holy Grail has been at the Cathedral since 1437. It is exhibited in the middle of an altar adorned in alabaster relief by Julià lo Florentí (Giuliano di Giovanni da Poggibonsi). It was brought to Valencia by influence of the Borgia lineage in the episcopate, the family that had put Callixtus III and Alexander VI in the Vatican.

The Romanesque Palace Portal and the majestic Gothic lantern tower

Keystone above the altar

Chapel of the Holy Grail

↑ **Plaça de la Mare de Déu (Square of Our Lady)**   ↓ **Basilica of Our Lady of the Abandoned (Mare de Déu dels Desemparats) – cupola**

Ciutat Vella | La Seu

Plaça de la Mare de Déu

The buildings in this pedestrian area are home to various institutions. Over the remains of the medieval city hall rises the seat of the Government of the Valencian Land, the Palau de la Generalitat Valenciana. Across from it is the church of the Our Lady of the Abandoned, patron saint of the city, and the cathedral (la Seu), metropolitan see of the archbishopric. Different celebrations over the course of the year fill this square with festivity, music and flowers.

The Palau de la Generalitat is a Gothic building representing regional political power. The large Gothic cathedral extols ecclesiastic power. The Basilica of Our Lady of the Abandoned is a focal point of popular devotion. The Neptune Fountain is a tribute to the network of irrigation channels devised by the Moors.

The Basilica is connected to the cathedral by a lofty renaissance arch. Here, *La Geperudeta* ('the little hunchback', endearing nickname given to the statue of Our Lady of the Abandoned) is worshipped. Always steeped in the aroma of flowers and incense, it was built between 1652 and 1667 by Diego Martínez Ponce. The precious vault is the work of Antonio Palomino.

Palau de la Generalitat

In the Mediterranean civil Gothic style, it is the seat of the Council and President of the Autonomous Community of Valencia. Pere Compte began construction in 1418, and works continued at different times until the mid-20th century. The Golden Hall, with its intricately-worked wooden, Renaissance coffered ceiling, and the Sala de Corts (Parliament Hall) are areas reserved for political and social activity. The central courtyard has large arches and a grand staircase.

Palau dels Borja

The Valencian Parliament (Corts Valencianes) is housed in the Palau or Palace of Benicarló or Palace of the Borgias. Originally the Duke of Gandia's palace in the city, the latest remodelling is by Manuel Portaceli and Carlos Salvadores. The garden hosts a ficus tree that's over 150 years old, as well as a cutting from the Anne Frank tree.

Palace of the Valencian Government (Palau de la Generalitat Valenciana)

Palace of the Borgias (Palau dels Borja)

Museu del Marqués de Campo

The Municipal Art Museum is located in a palace built for the Dukes of Villahermosa in the 18th century across from the Archbishop's Palace. When the Royal Palace was destroyed, the building became headquarters of the Captaincy General. It later became the residence of the former mayor, the Marquis of Campo. The museum exhibits the municipal art collection and hosts temporary exhibitions.

Archbishop's Palace

This palace was designed by Vicente Traver in 1941 to substitute the one burnt down in 1936. The style is Neobaroque historicism with reminiscences of the Seville Baroque, very different to the architectural styles typical of the area. The brick façade consists of a mezzanine floor with tall windows, a main floor with balconies and a prominent central area with ornamentation. The archbishop's residence is connected to the cathedral by a bridge over Barxilla Street.

Palau del Marqués de Campo (Marquis of Campo Palace)

Archbishop's Palace and arch over Carrer de la Barcella

L'Almodí

When Valencia was under Moorish rule, this granary was created to keep the city supplied. Revamped in the 15th century, it has a basilican floor plan with three naves. Formerly the Palaeontology Museum, it is now used as a municipal exhibit hall. The word *almodí* translates to a unit of measurement for weight.

L'Almoina Museum and Archaeological Site

The city began to exist here when the Romans founded Valentia (138 BC). The Museum displays urban vestiges from Roman, Visigoth and Moorish times. Under the Plaça de Dècim Juni Brut, a Roman military commander credited with founding the city, are the remains of the Roman baths and streets, the Visigoth basilica and the Moorish *alcàsser* or palace. These ruins were discovered in an excavation in 1985. The word *almoina* means charitable institution and refers to a medieval centre for the poor that used to stand on this site.

Crypt of Saint Vincent Martyr

Located on the ground floor of a *Modernista* building, it was part of a Visigoth cathedral. According to tradition, the saint was imprisoned and died here (304 AD). The body of the first Valencian martyr was moved to the extramural neighbourhood or raval of Sant Vicent de la Roqueta, where Mozarabs, i.e. Christians living under Muslim rule, continued to worship the saint.

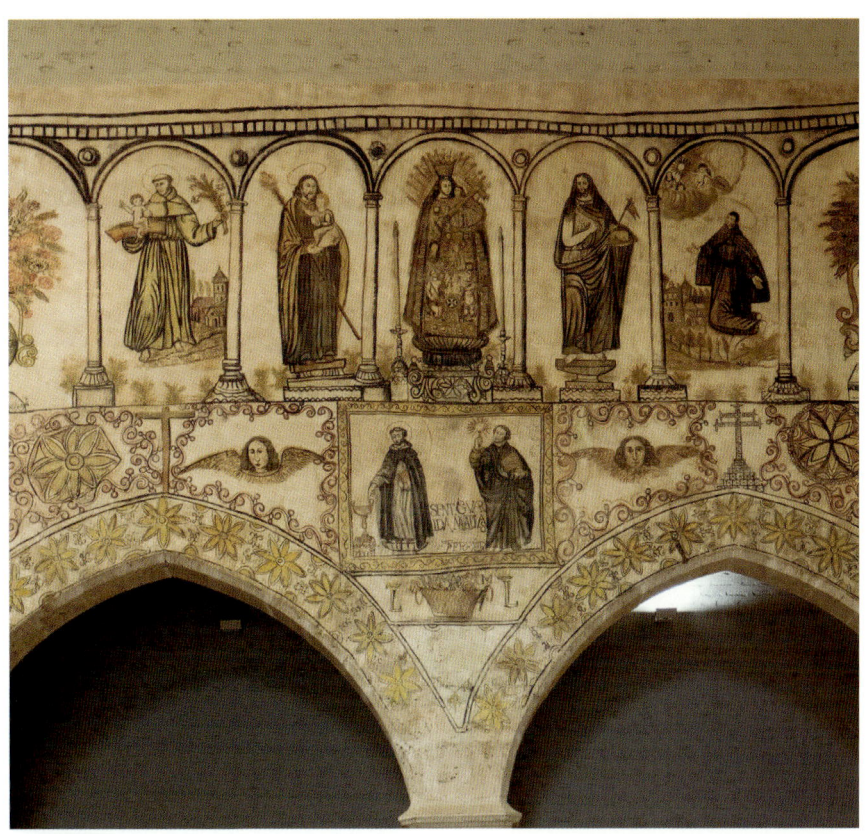

L'Almodí

Crypt of Saint Vincent Martyr

L'Almoina Archaeological Centre

↑ **Carrer dels Cavallers** ↓ Mercader Palace courtyard

Ciutat Vella | La Seu

Carrer dels Cavallers

This is one of the main streets leading into the historic heart of the city. It has kept the urban elegance of its Gothic and Baroque palaces intact (Fuentehermosa, Malferit, Alpont, Centelles). One of the residential areas preferred by the Valencian nobility, its narrow breadth evokes the dark atmosphere of some of the streets in Barcelona and Palma de Mallorca's Gothic Quarters. The spectacular courtyards provide a backdrop for some of the lively nightlife in bars, taverns and restaurants attending to many of the city's visitors. The flourishing Valencia of the 15th and 16th centuries found its best showcase for courtesan and refined lifestyles in this street. It also serves as one of the exits towards the area to the west of the capital.

Negret, Correu Vell and Sant Nicolau Squares

With a steady flow of pedestrians from Carrer dels Cavallers, the Plaça del Negret is a great place to have a drink out-of-doors. It is named after the sculpture on the fountain, the first one to supply potable water to the Old City as of 1850.

Correu Vell is another of the small squares accompanying Carrer dels Cavallers. It is quiet because there are no terraces. This plaza was already present on the first city map, drawn up by father Tosca in 1704. The sacristy of Saint Nicolau Church extends its façade up to this square. The church's main portal opens onto another small plaza named after the church.

Negret Square

Correu Vell Square

Sant Nicolau Square

Ciutat Vella | La Seu

Church of Sant Nicolau and Sant Pere Màrtir

After its recent restoration, it is one of the most beautiful Gothic-Baroque churches in Valencia. The magnificent splendour of the original paintings, executed by Dionís Vidal according to a design by Antonio Palomino on the long, vaulted ceiling and now very finely restored, allow it to be referred to as the city's Little Sistine Chapel.

Although it was one of the first seven churches established after the 13th century Christian conquest in the place where a mosque once stood, it was always a remarkably wealthy parish because it was on the street where the nobility lived. It thus managed to expand its surface area and spaces of worship. It underwent its first reform in 1455, when Jaume Roig, a poet and medical doctor, was responsible for its conservation.

The second reform occurred in the late 17th century with a Baroque intervention by the architect Pérez Castiel, who kept the Gothic vault intact, in contrast to other churches in the city, which were covering them at the time. It was during this reform that the vault paintings depicting the lives and miracles of the two patron saints, Saint Peter Martyr and Saint Nicholas of Bari, were done. Over the door of the Communion Chapel, Dionís Vidal painted a portrait of his master as a tribute, and Antonio Palomino did the same for his disciple.

The church's floor plan is simple, typical of early Gothic. It shares several walls with adjoining palaces and homes, and it is thus blocked from view from Carrer Cavallers.

Saint Nicholas of Bari

Baroque frescos on the Gothic vault

La Xerea

This neighbourhood has a more tranquil and roomier atmosphere than that of la Seu. Its streets are also laid out in more rational fashion. There is a significant number of convents, upper middle class homes and palaces restored by the Administration.

From Carrer de les Avellanes, it extends east towards the Glorieta Gardens, Plaça de Tetuan and the former citadel. It is bordered by the Túria Gardens to the north, and the shopping street of Carrer de la Pau to the south. In the past, there was a Jewish neighbourhood here and the Moorish quarters, with their own marketplace and cemeteries. The word *xerea* comes from the Arabic word *sharia*, which in this case means path leading to the neighbourhoods located outside the city walls.

Its traditional main street was Carrer de la Mar until Carrer de la Pau was opened up. The main park is La Glorieta. It was the first public garden in the city, created during the French occupation in the early 19th century, and eventually boasted all the necessary paraphernalia for citizens to enjoy their leisure: a fountain with a grotto, a café, a bandstand and an open-air theatre enclosed by a fence. Its monumental trees are remarkable.

Of the significant heritage the city had during the centuries of Moorish occupation, the only thing left standing in this neighbourhood is an important monument: the Banys de l'Almirall (Admiral's Baths), a medieval building used as a public steam bath, with three vaulted halls.

Church of Saint Stephen, lateral façade

Admiral's Baths

Bench in the Glorieta Gardens

Església de Sant Esteve
(Church of Saint Stephen)

The Church of Saint Stephen is one of the ten parishes consecrated in 1238, after the Christian conquest of Valencia. The current temple is the result of a Baroque intervention and a subsequent Neoclassical one. Tradition dictates that the daughters of El Cid were married and Saint Vincent Ferrer baptised here.

Palau del Temple
(Palace of the Templars)

The building now housing the Spanish Government's Delegation to the Valencian Community occupies what used to be a monastery built by the Knights Templar. Under Charles III of Spain, its architecture was transformed to bring it into the purest, 18th-century Academic style, especially evident in the cloister and its columns. This was the compensation the monarch gave the Order of Montesa, whose headquarters in a town south of Valencia had been destroyed by an earthquake. In the same building, the order also had a school and a church in annex, whose façade is a tribute to the Bourbon kings and the Catholic religion. Inside are important frescos by Josep Vergara.

Reial Convent de Sant Doménec
(Royal Monastery of Saint Dominic)

It was the most important monastery in the city in the 18th century. When the Dominican monastery was closed due to Spain's Ecclesiastic Confiscations, the grounds, which have a view of the sea, were given over to the Captaincy General (the regional military command) to perpetuate the defensive nature of this eastern corner of the city.

The architectural ensemble has brilliant examples of different periods. The Royal Chapel, in Mediterranean Gothic, was built by the Valencian Kings Alphons the Magnanimous and John II. The central, marble sepulchre dedicated to the Marquises of Zenete is next to the remains of the Valencian Renaissance painter Joan de Joanes. The monastery has two cloisters: a Gothic one and a cloister from the Renaissance.

Knights Templar Monastery from the Túria Gardens

Sepulchre of the Marquises of Zenete, Saint Dominic Royal Monastery

Carrer de la Mar

Together with Carrer dels Cavallers, this is one of the most elegant streets in the city. It once led to the city gates at the Pont del Mar, a bridge over the river, connecting the city to the port area.

Before the rival Carrer de la Pau emerged at the turn of the 20th century, all carriage and foot traffic moving towards the eastern part of the city would circulate on this slightly curved street, which was a bit wider than the medieval Cavallers. The city's chronicler, Vicent Boix, wrote in 1863 that it was sometimes called *carrer matjor de la Mar* (Main Street [to] the Sea).

Sant Joan de l'Hospital
(Saint John of Jerusalem)

This Knights Hospitaller architectural complex is another of the significant monasteries in La Xerea. The Opus Dei has recovered it for worship after it had been used as a cinema. James I of Aragon granted this church to the Order of Malta in gratitude for their collaboration in the reconquest of Valencia. The Gothic temple has a small chapel consecrated to Saint Barbara and containing the remains of a Byzantine empress who took refuge in Valencia thanks to the protection of Valencian King Peter III of Aragon, known as Peter the Great. Along this fringe area lay the Muslim part of medieval Valencia.

Ornamentation, Marquis of Valero de Palma Palace (Carrer de la Mar)

Saint John of Jerusalem, north portal

Saint John of Jerusalem, nave

Birth Home of Saint Vincent Ferrer

Known as *El pouet de Sant Vicent* (Saint Vincent's little well), this is the ancestral home of the Ferrer family, where the patron saint of the city was born. At a side entrance next to the chapel where this popular missionary is worshipped, the water from a small well is offered in memory of his miracles, depicted on interesting Manises ceramic tile murals.

Palau de Cervelló

Official residence of the Spanish monarchs in Valencia during the 19th century after the Royal Palace was torn down, the Palace of the Counts of Cervelló now houses the Municipal Historic Archives. On the 'noble floor' (*planta noble*), there is an interesting reconstruction of the atmosphere of 19th-century salons, though the floor dates back to the 16th century. In the early 19th century, Felipe Osorio Castellví, Count of Cervelló and General of the Valencian Forces of the Spanish Army, moved to Madrid, ceding the palace to the government for public use.

Palau del Senyor de Bétera
(Palace of the Lord of Bétera)

The Palace of the Lord of Bétera and that of the Marquis of Dosaigües were spared from demolition when the area around the former university was redeveloped. This building, also known as the Palace of the Boïl d'Arenós Family, is currently the seat of the Valencia Stock Exchange. The former central courtyard, Gothic in origin, now hosts stock exchange and procurement activities.

Birth home of Saint Vincent Ferrer

Palace of the Boïl d'Arenós Family

Cervelló Palace

Palau del Marqués de Dosaigües
(Palace of the Marquis of Dosaigües)

This building's claim to fame is its spectacular Baroque portal. The Palace of the Marquis of Dosaigües has housed the González Martí National Ceramics Museum since 1954, which offers a thorough look at the history of ceramic art. Using Manuel González Martí's original collection, the first floor recreates life in an 18th-19th century palace, as well as bourgeois domestic life and customs. Other rooms are dedicated to the collections of Manises, Alcora and Paterna ceramics, a significant catalogue of 15th-century glazed ceramic tiles (*rajola de València* or *azulejos*) and *socarrats* (glazed tiles decorated in a "burnt" style), Chinese porcelain and traditional pottery from Andalusia and Toledo.

The façade is a true work of art. In the mid-18th century, the Valencian painter and engraver, Hipòlit Rovira, was commissioned for the job, and he retained Ignasi Vergara to carve the alabaster work on the magnificent portal. The upper area depicts Our Lady of the Rosary, while the lower is an allegory of two rivers (in reference to the Marquis' name, Dosaigües, i.e. Two Waters), represented by two bald giants, one nude and the other slightly clothed, whose bodies are entwined with plant and animal motifs, resulting in a highly sensual sculptural whole.

The palace has experienced a number of transformations. Beginning in 1740, it was remodelled to improve its courtly aspect. The large portal was added, the corner tower was duplicated and the balconies endowed with carved stone balustrades.

The 1870 remodelling was done by master José Ferrer. To prevent humidity seeping in, the façades were lined in imitation-marble panels, and Rococo and Neo-imperial ornamentation was added. The building's conventional style is far removed from the magnificent fantasy applied exclusively to the façade.

← Above: The spectacular façade
Below: Kitchen in the Ceramics Museum

The alabaster giants on the Baroque portal

Ballroom

Ciutat Vella | La Xerea

Church and College of the Patriarch

This architectural complex was founded by Saint John de Ribera as a seminary in the spirit of the Counterreformation in the face of Protestantism. The cloister, with its two-tiered colonnade (the best Renaissance work in the city), is a must, as is the church in Herrerian style, with paintings by Francesc Ribalta. The "dragon" or "lizard" hanging in the vestibule was a gift from the Viceroy of Peru, although local popular legend recounts that it arrived along Carrer de les Barques when an arm of the river flowed through the area.

The founder held the positions of Viceroy of the Kingdom of Valencia, Commander in Chief, (Latin) Patriarch of Antioch and Chancellor of the University. His influence before the king of Spain was decisive in the 1609 expulsion of the *moriscos* (converted Muslims).

The Patriarch chose this location to counteract the dissemination of scientific secularism being taught by university professors.

La Nau

Lluís Vives, the universal humanist born in Valencia, presides over the cloister in this university building dedicated to the dissemination of knowledge. Its historical library holds the first book printed in Spain (1474), about the Virgin Mary. The main façade, remodelled in modern times, is a tribute to the Borgia Pope, Alexander VI, and to King Ferdinand II, because they granted Valencia the privilege of having one of the first European universities.

Carrer de la Pau

This is possibly the most architecturally artistic street in the city. All of its buildings have heritage status. The street was laid out in the late 19th century. The prosperous local bourgeoisie took up residence in large buildings. In the 1920s, it was modern and bustling, sporting hotels, restaurants and shops. It leads from the inner ring route to the historic centre and is particularly known for its travel agencies, fashion boutiques and restaurants.

← El Patriarca complex, church cupola and cloister

La Nau, central courtyard

Carrer de la Pau

Ciutat Vella | El Carme

El Carme

El Carme was historically a neighbourhood of craftspeople, monasteries, and the residence of nobility and the middle class. It is now a focal point for art and fashion, the heritage of the Fine Arts School that once graced these quarters. It is a mixed-income area, as traditional palaces stand next to middle-class homes and rental flats. The decadence that began in 1957, after a major flood of the River Túria, ended in the late 1970s when the area became popular among young people. At present, local artists prefer the opportunities afforded by Russafa, while visitors often choose El Carme for its old-town atmosphere and bohemian image.

It takes its name from the Carme Monastery, which is now an art exhibit hall. Its perimeter has two gates to the medieval city walls and follows the streets Serrans, Cavallers and Quart, continuing along the Ronda Guillem de Castro and Blanqueries on the right bank of the Túria Gardens.

Torres dels Serrans

The Serrans Towers were the northern entrance gate to the city, built by architect Pere Balaguer beginning in 1391. The gate consists of two pentagonal towers connected by a wall, topped by battlements and sporting a continuous gallery of machicolations, further defended by a moat. It continues to be used as one of the main entrances to the Old City.

Its monumentality and Gothic elegance were designed to impress political delegations visiting the city. The Royal Gates to Poblet Monastery in Catalonia look like a small-scale replica. They served as a prison for noblemen. In 1936, paintings from Madrid's Prado Museum were stashed here to protect them from bombardment or damage during the Spanish Civil War.

Casa de les Roques

Building where the *Roques* are kept, i.e. floats used during Corpus Christi, once the city's main feast day before it was eclipsed by the Falles. The floats are pulled by local teams of horses. On them, the Mysteries of Corpus were acted out.

← Serrans Towers

Gargoyles on the Serrans Towers

Roques, **giants and beasts at rest at the Casa de les Roques**

Plaça del Carme (Carme Square)

An urban area of architectural interest, this plaza was created to show off the Carme Monastery's church façade. The temple's Baroque style matches that of the Palau de l'Intendent Pineda (Palace of Quartermaster Pineda), home to the UIMP (Universidad Internacional Menéndez Pelayo). This palace was inaugurated in 1732, three years before its owner, Francesc Salvador de Pineda, was expelled from the city under the accusation of corruption and abuse of office. Pineda was the tax collector for the Kingdoms of Valencia and Murcia. In the middle of the square is a sculpture of the Valencian Renaissance painter, Joan de Joanes.

Centre del Carme Museum

After Disentailment (*Desamortización*, i.e. Spain's Ecclesiastic Confiscations) in the early 19th century, the Discalced Carmelites left this monastery, which had been functioning since 1280. Under the criteria of the Sant Carles Academy, it became the School of Fine Arts and Provincial Museum. The monastery's different halls, in various styles, host significant exhibits. The Gothic cloister radiates strength and a classical atmosphere. The Renaissance cloister, steeped in vegetation, transmits a sense of intimacy. The great Sala Ferreras, known as "la Academia", the Aula Capitular (Chapter Hall), the Refectory, Goerlich Hall, and even the monks' dormitory provide space for exhibits of any style.

Casa Museu Josep Benlliure (Josep Benlliure House Museum)

Within these walls lived one of the great artists of the late 19th century. Located on the inner ring road around the Old City, it shows the style of a typical Valencian bourgeois home, with four floors and an inner garden that inspired the artist. His studio was at the rear of the garden. Benlliure, together with Sorolla and Pinazo, are the greatest representatives of 19th-century Valencian painting. The building is in Eclectic Style, with ornamentation of Greco-Roman influence.

← Plaça del Carme

Cloister, Centre del Carme Museum

Studio, Josep Benlliure House Museum

NOSTRA DONA
DE LA BONA SON
PRESUEU PER NOS
PORTAL
DE VALLDIGNA

Ciutat Vella | El Carme

Carrer dels Cavallers

This elegant street is filled with Gothic palaces and shares the atmospheres of both El Carme and La Seu. Before it was settled by the city's notable families, it was a Roman road entering from the west. A similar use was made by the Moors. At the end of Cavallers Street, next to Sant Jaume Square, was the *alfòndec*, a complex for merchants trading with the Crown of Aragon that included a warehouse, lodgings and a trading area. The proximity to this trading point may have been a factor attracting landlords to build their mansions here. Each year on Corpus Christi, a large processional monstrance is carried down this street under an intense shower of rose petals thrown by the neighbours from their balconies.

Plaça del Tossal (Tossal Square) is the point where Cavallers, Bosseria and Quart Streets meet. It is called *Tossal* or Hill because it sits on higher ground, and for centuries held back the waters of the Túria branch that flowed by this part of the city. This branch of the river was used as a moat for the Moorish city walls. It was later covered and became the Rovella canal, the city's principal sewer mains. This information can be discovered in a museum under the plaza, where you can see the 13th-century Moorish ramparts. At Cavallers 36 and Col·legi Major Rector Peset, other sections of the Moorish walls can still be seen.

Portal de la Valldigna
(Valldigna City Gates)

This gate was opened in the Moorish walls to create a new entrance to the extramural *moreria* or Moorish Quarters located next to the river. In the 15th century, it lost its wooden door, since the Christian wall further north already provided security. The remains of the Moorish city walls attain a spectacular thickness here. The Gothic panel painting over the gate depicts James II founding the monastery of Santa Maria de la Valldigna.

← Portal de la Valldigna

Plaça de Sant Jaume (Saint James Square)

Plaça de l'Espart (Esparto Square), next to Carrer dels Cavallers

Quart Towers

Stairs leading to the towers

Carrer de Quart

This modern street is an extension of Carrer dels Cavallers with 19th century bourgeois homes and other more popular buildings housing artisans and their workshops. One of the most prominent buildings is Edificio Echeveste, built in Eclectic style by Joaquín Calvo, home to Renaissance writers Rafael Ferrer i Bigné and Manuel Millàs Casanoves. The street was built on the extensive land of the Purity Convent (Convent de la Puritat).

Torres de Quart
(Quart Towers)

This city gate was built in the western section of the city walls from 1441 to 1460 by Pere Bonfill to allow entry of trade and travellers from the Iberian hinterland. It consists of twin towers with a u-shaped floor plan, cylindrical towards the front and straight at the rear. The entrance gate is a rounded arch topped by a gallery of machicolations. You can still see the marks left on the façade by the impacts of cannonballs fired by the French army in 1808. These towers served as a prison for women, which allowed them to remain standing when the majority of gates to the city were torn down.

Santa Úrsula
(Saint Ursula)

Temple belonging to the former Augustinian Convent built in 1605, which had a home for 'repentant women'. This is yet another building confirming the convent-monasterial origins of the Carme Neighbourhood. It currently houses part of the Catholic University of Valencia.

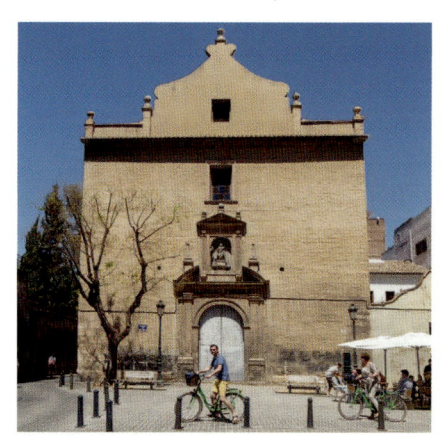

Church of Saint Ursula

IVAM

The Valencian Institute of Modern Art (Institut Valencià d'Art Modern) is a museum in a modern building called Centre Julio González, named after the great European avant-garde sculptor who was a contemporary of Picasso. The staircase connecting the ground floor with the first and second floors is the museum's most spectacular architectural element, together with the large façade windows.

The permanent collection focuses on the European avant-garde, the world of photography and graphic art, as well as contemporary sculpture and installations faithful to the founding spirit of tribute to Julio González. European Informalism, Abstract Expressionism, Pop Art and Realism are well represented at the IVAM, not to mention the Valencian Modern painting of Ignasi Pinazo, Joaquim Sorolla and Francesc Lozano.

IVAM lobby

Julio González, *Femme au miroir* (1936-37)

IVAM exhibit hall

↑ La Beneficència - its former Neo-Byzantine church   ↓ Ethnology Museum

Ciutat Vella | El Carme

Centre Cultural La Beneficència

A large building designed by the architect Joaquín María Belda Ibáñez in 1876, it has recently become the second major 'cultural container' in the area. This vast construction with eight courtyards was a hospice in the 19th century, providing a space for social services and charity work run by the Valencian Provincial Council or Diputació. It's main architectural lines are Neogothic and Neobyzantine. At present, after renovations in 1994, seven years after the construction of the IVAM, it hosts the province's Prehistory and Ethnology Museums and features some remarkable temporary exhibits relating to the Valencian lifestyle and worldview.

Extramural Quart Street

Just as Carrer dels Cavallers was extended by the name of Carrer de Quart, this street was further extended beyond the city walls, with farms and gardens on either side. One of the most significant was the Hort de Tramoieres (Tramoieres' Garden or Orchard). In the 18th century, a church was built that lent urban cohesion to this extramural neighbourhood.

Jardí Botànic (Botanical Garden)

One of the city's extramural gardens along Quart Street, spanning four hectares, became a Gardening School by initiative of the University of Valencia. It was naturalist Antoni Josep Cavanilles who, in the mid-19th century, redesigned this garden to lend it the characteristics of a scientific one, with over 3,000 species of trees and plants. Architect Cristòfol Sales designed the botanical garden's original layout. The emblematic umbracle or shaded greenhouse by Arturo Mélida opened its doors in 1900.

Annexed to the garden, a small botanical jewel has recently been created, the Jardí de les Hespèrides (Garden of the Hesperides), where fifty varieties of citrus grow. It is a tribute to the traditional gardeners of the 15th and 16th centuries.

Botanical Garden research building

Shaded greenhouse or umbracle

Ciutat Vella | El Mercat

El Mercat

Valencia has succeeded in differentiating the urban area where the soul and politics are cultivated from the neighbourhood where people try to make a living, do business and eat and make merry. While la Seu represents an arena for the Church and politics, El Mercat (the Marketplace) is a platform for civil and citizen power and their commercial arts.

Mercat Central
(Central Market Hall)

The *Modernista* architects, Francesc Guàrdia and Alexandre Soler, disciples of Lluís Domènech i Montaner, built the Central Market Hall between 1914 and 1928, coinciding with a period of growth for Valencia. They demonstrated that industrial materials could be fused with bold ornamental elements. Under a monumental roof of iron and glass, two hundred stalls selling fresh produce and other food compete on a daily basis with the city's shops.

One of the most striking features in this surface area of over 8,000 square meters freed from its former monasterial and housing uses is the specialised fish and seafood section and the many exotic stands designed to provide great pleasure to the taste buds. On the impressive cupula is a weathervane known as *la cotorra del Mercat* (the Market parrot), an emblematic item that has been cited in literary works such as *sainets* (theatrical comedy sketches) and novels.

The Market Square and surroundings were commercial centres in medieval Valencia, even in Moorish times, though this was an extramural area. Writer Vicente Blasco Ibáñez describes the marketplace atmosphere in his novels, where farmers, traders, sellers, buyers, the curious, peddlers and hagglers all mixed, many struggling for a space for their merchandise. The city council decided to build the large market hall to regulate the chaos of stands, awnings, peddlers' carts and horses that would occupy the square and the neighbourhood's narrow streets every morning.

← Cupola and façade of the Central Market Hall

The Market Parrot (*La cotorra del Mercat*), an emblematic weathervane

The monumental iron and glass ceiling

↑ Paella pans for sale at a stall outside the market   ↓ Urban art nearby

Ciutat Vella | El Mercat

Around the Market Hall

The Market Hall square boasts three emblematic buildings of civil and religious architecture that make Valencia a highly valued artistic destination: the remarkable gothic of the Silk Exchange (Llotja de la Seda), the *Modernista* Central Market Hall (Mercat Central) and the Baroque Church of Saint John (Església de Sant Joan del Mercat).

Outside the market hall, you can taste typical products and purchase anything from a paella pan to a souvenir. The old café-bars and shops add authenticity to this picturesque scene.

Valencia awakens to the arrival of fresh produce from the area being unloaded into the market. The first tuna or calamari sandwiches of the day are eaten at the bars. Foods are organized at stalls to look appealing, as if they were freshly painted still lifes.

Orxateria (tiger nut parlour) outside the market hall

Commercial decoration on the pavement

Hat shop

Makeshift snail and rosemary stand

Ciutat Vella | El Mercat

La Llotja de la Seda (Silk Exchange)

Declared a UNESCO World Heritage Site, the Silk Exchange is the most beautiful and significant secular Gothic building in Valencia. Within its walls, intense commercial and financial activity took place. Construction, begun in 1483 by master Pere Compte, was fully paid by the Taula de Canvis, the first Valencian banking institution. It is therefore an artistic tribute to the virtues of money.

The Hall of Columns consists of a forest of twenty-four helicoidal columns that fan out like palm leaves upon reaching the ceiling. Tables with stools were placed amid these 17.4-meter-high columns, tables marked with the name of the owner executing the sales and purchase transactions. The central tower includes a small chapel and a 110-step spiral staircase leading to a prison for bankrupt traders. From the Pati dels Tarongers, a courtyard with a fountain in the middle surrounded by orange trees where the public entrance is located, a steep stone staircase leads to the Meeting Hall of the Consulate of the Sea, a judicial body administering maritime and commercial law. This is a sumptuous hall whose carved and painted, coffered ceiling was originally in the early Valencian city hall at Plaça de la Mare de Déu.

Anthropomorphic and zoomorphic gargoyles, suggestive sculptures and medallions all bespeak the medieval symbolism and fantasy contained in the Llotja's artwork.

Silk Exchange tower and crenellations

Coat of arms of the Kingdom of Valencia

Intricately decorated woodwork, ceiling of the Consulate of the Sea

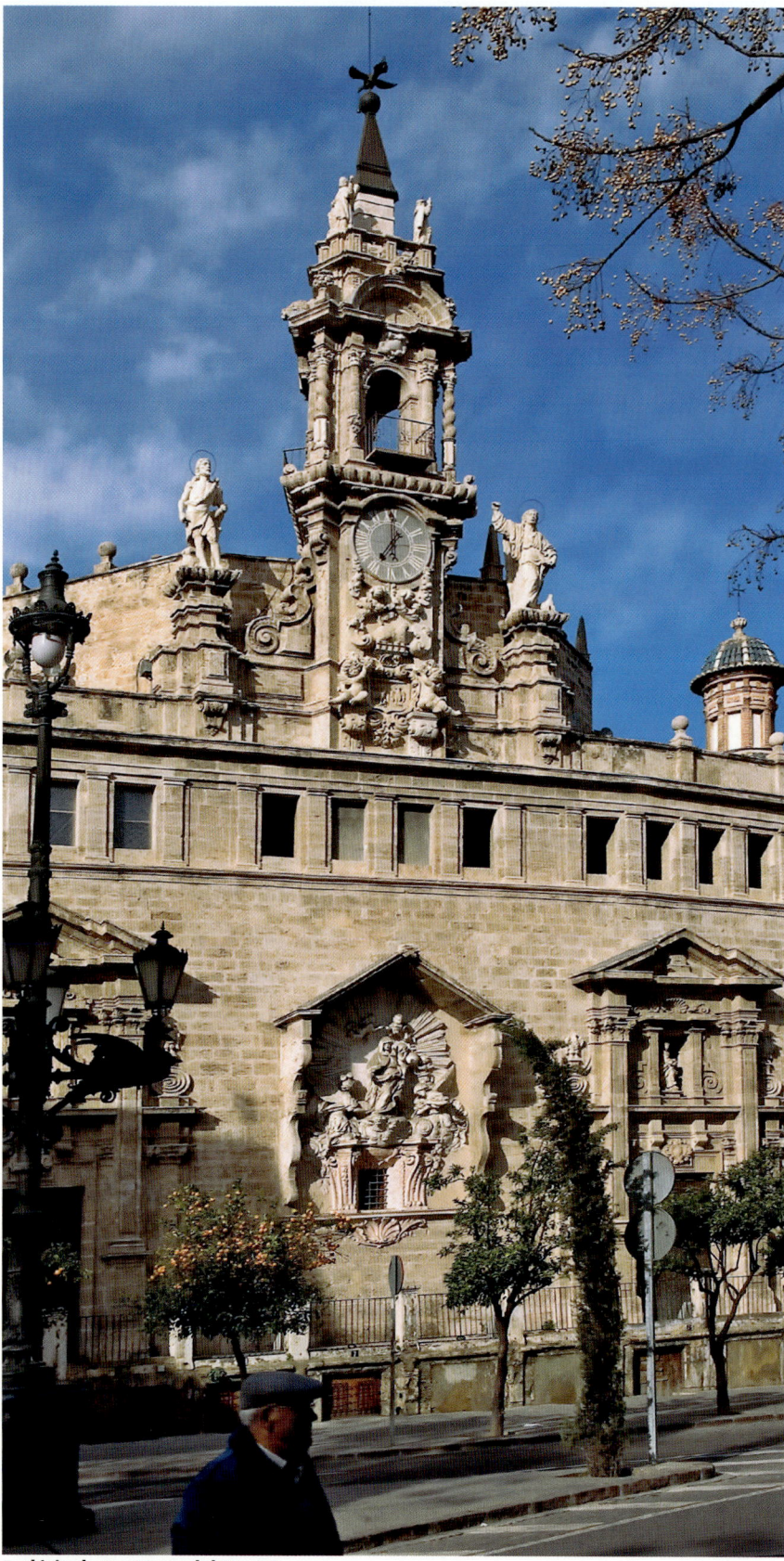

Església de Sant Joan del Mercat

The Church of Saints John (dedicated to John the Evangelist and John the Baptist) was built over a former mosque in Gothic style, but was thoroughly redesigned in the 18th century and turned into a Baroque-style building. The frontispiece visible from Market Square actually conceals the former Gothic polygonal apse behind its flat façade. A striking element of this area is a terrace that was used as a large balcony from which to watch major celebrations such as the Corpus procession. The Apocalypse frescoes by Antonio Palomino are one of the most remarkable elements of the interior. The weathervane on the tower represents the eagle of the Apocalypse, though urban legend has dubbed it Saint John's sparrow.

Streets and squares with trades

The city is full of small streets and plazas where shops attract throngs of buyers. A stroll through Mercè Square and Carrer del Músic Peydró provides an interesting opportunity to peruse the concentration of traditional shops selling furniture and other objects made of wood and natural fibres (wicker, straw, reed). Other areas revolve around antiquarians and antique books shops. Street names evoke artisan trades: Bosseria (bag-makers), Cadirers (chair-makers), Assaonadors (tanners), Manyans (Locksmiths), Tapineria (sandal-makers), etc.

Plaça Redona

The Round Plaza is the most popular square in the area. It was built between 1839 and 1856 to offer a single market space for the fish, meat and produce being sold throughout the narrow streets of the Mercat neighbourhood, well before the Modernista market hall was planned. This was also the point when the district abattoir was moved to a more hygienic facility outside the city walls. The central fountain was cherished during the marketplace period. The plaza is like a small bullring, filled with craft shops as well as flats. Recent in-depth remodelling has excessively modified its traditional aspect.

Església de Sant Joan del Mercat

↑ **The popular Round Plaza (Plaça Redona)**   ↓ **Wickerwork shop on Carrer del Músic Peydró**

Sant Francesc

In the mid-19th century, the City Council decided to leave its age-old location at Plaça de la Mare de Déu and build a new city hall in the southeast quarter of the medieval city, occupied by monasteries and popular housing. The neighbourhood takes its name from the monastery formerly at the central square. This is a neighbourhood of great bourgeois architecture, finances, local government, theatres, cinemas and designer shops.

Plaça de l'Ajuntament

This triangular square has the tallest buildings in the Old City, projected by the best architects of the early 20th century. Francesc Mora and Carlos Carbonell expanded the Casa de l'Ensenyança (a former charitable institution for children) into the Town Hall (Ajuntament), with façade on the plaza. They sought an image combining typical local architecture with Classic elements and Renaissance and Baroque ornamentation. The Balcony of the Authorities, where the population's gaze falls during local festivities, was added more recently.

A marble staircase leads to the Crystal Hall. To the right is the Hemicycle or Council Chamber and other halls with a distinguished collection of artworks on their walls. The Municipal History Museum that shares a part of this building displays objects relating to the city's identity: the flag of the Valencian Land, James I's sword, the *Furs de València* (incunabulum edition of the Kingdom of Valencia's lawcode), the Pennon of the Conquest and the earliest map of the city of Valencia.

Emblematic buildings on Plaça de l'Ajuntament (Town Council Square)

Typical flower stand

Municipal History Museum, Hall of the *Furs* (medieval Valencian law code)

Passatge Ripalda

This small arcade was built in 1889 by Joaquín María Arnau, an architect of the Valencian Romantic school. It's a shopping arcade in a residential building with two façades, covered by a steel and glass vault in a small-scale imitation of Milan's glorious Galleria Vittorio Emanuele.

Edifici de Correos

The Central Post Office Building, designed by Miguel Ángel Navarro Pérez and inaugurated in 1923, was intended to rival the Town Hall in monumentality. It is a tribute to the social progress represented by postal and telegraph communications. Inside is a spectacular oval hall with Ionic columns and a large glass cupola with the coats of arms of Spain's different regions. The royal coat of arms of Spain presides over the façade, which is further adorned with sculptures of angels, utopian emissaries connecting the continents by land and air. The architect followed an academic style to avoid the more traditional, old-fashioned look of the other buildings on the large square.

Rialto Building

Architect Cayetano Borso di Carminati applied a rationalist style with Art Deco influences to this 1930s building. It began as a cinema, but during the (post-Franco) Transition, it added the function of theatre thanks to renovation by the Generalitat. It houses the Film Archive of the Valencian Land.

Central Post Office building with its emblematic communications tower

Rialto Building

← **Ripalda Arcade**

Lion postboxes on the Post Office building

Carrer de Sant Vicent Màrtir

Lateral façade of Saint Martin's Church

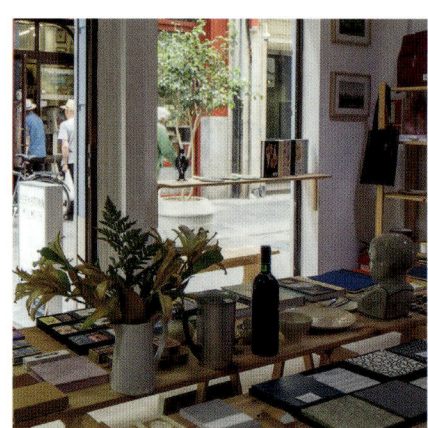

Shop on Carrer de Sant Ferran

Carrer de Sant Vicent Màrtir

This is one of the longest and most traditional streets of the medieval city, which by 1900 was a bustling shopping street. It was extended beyond the city walls, which makes it the street with the greatest number of buildings in Valencia. Specialists say the Valencian Route of the Saint James Way began here.

Església de Sant Martí (Saint Martin's Church)

This early Gothic church was erected over a former mosque in 1382. In the 18th century it was renovated in Baroque style. The façade boasts an important sculptural group by the Flemish artist, Pieter Van Beckere, representing the saint helping a pauper. The Communion Chapel has an independent entrance from a small plaza.

Carrer de Sant Ferran

This street is full of traditional shops (used books, antiques, herb shops, hand-crafted fashion), sharing space with modern cafés and *tascas* (Spanish pubs or bistros). The Octubre Centre de Cultura Contemporània restored a 19th-century department store, El Siglo Valenciano, transforming it into a cultural venue. In the basement, you can see remains of the Moorish city walls.

Ciutat Vella | Sant Francesc

Banco de Valencia
In 1940, Xavier Goerlich, Antonio Gómez Davó and Vicente Traver were commissioned to construct a building for the Bank of Valencia that would represent Valencian financial power. Its location on a chamfered street corner lends it greater visibility than true heritage value. It is an example of Neo-Valencian style with Renaissance and Baroque elements.

Teatre Principal
The most elegant and emblematic theatre in the city, it was inaugurated in 1832. Designed by the Italian Filippo Fontana as a venue for the great productions of the time, it has a Neoclassical façade.

Palau de Justícia
This former Customs House is located at the area where goods once arrived from the port. It was later a tobacco factory, and in the 20th century, became a justice administration building. Plaça d'Alfons El Magnànim honours James I of Aragon with a statue in the centre.

Former Bank of Valencia headquarters

Teatre Principal

Palace of Justice, former Customs House

A hall in the College of High Silk Art

Artistic silk fabric

Col·legi de l'Art Major de la Seda
(College of High Silk Art)

The former neighbourhood of Velluters (Velvet-Makers), now called El Pilar, was host to the silk industry for several centuries. Indeed, from the 15th until the mid-19th, it was one of the city's most important economic activities.

With the exception of the Escola Pia and this building, the neighbourhood lacks other monuments of notable architecture. The urban fabric consists of long, narrow streets, where the ground floors of buildings were often given over to artisan silkwork, although the looms were usually on the upper floors. Silkworms were raised on extramural farms, using the water from the Rovella irrigation channel that ran through the area.

The silk guild, founded in 1477, was the city's most influential social group. This is why the guild headquarters, purchased in 1492, retains the elements of an institution of historical importance. The archive has 660 books and 48 codices containing membership changes and guild agreements.

Parts of the building are now open to the public. You can visit the Sala de la Pometa (Little Apple Hall), with ceramic floor tiling from Sagunt, the Saló de la Fama (Hall of Fame), with remarkable floor tiling representing four continents, the chapel, the Gothic spiral staircase, a museum with silk pieces from the 17th and 18th centuries, and a workshop with functioning looms.

Shop

Ciutat Vella | Velluters

Jardins de l'antic Hospital (Former Hospital Gardens)

One of the first asylums in Europe, later converted into a regular hospital, was once located here. The only elements remaining are the four naves with ribbed vaults of the infirmary, now a library. When the rest of the facilities were torn down in 1960, after they had served as Faculty of Medicine, a garden was created, with Renaissance architectural ruins and cultural facilities.

Architect Guillermo Vázquez Consuegra designed the area's emblematic modern building, the MuVIM (the Valencian Museum of Illustration and Modernity), run by the Diputació (Valencia Provincial Council). It does not have its own collection, but hosts major temporary exhibits on design, poster art, photography and the Council's art holdings.

The Crafts Centre showcases woodworking, ceramics and papier-mâché, among many other handcrafted objects. The Saint Lucia chapel was attached to the hospital.

Saint Lucy Chapel

Public Provincial Library with cupola

Crafts Centre

Model of the city, Valencian Museum of Illustration and Modernity

L'Eixample
Modernisme

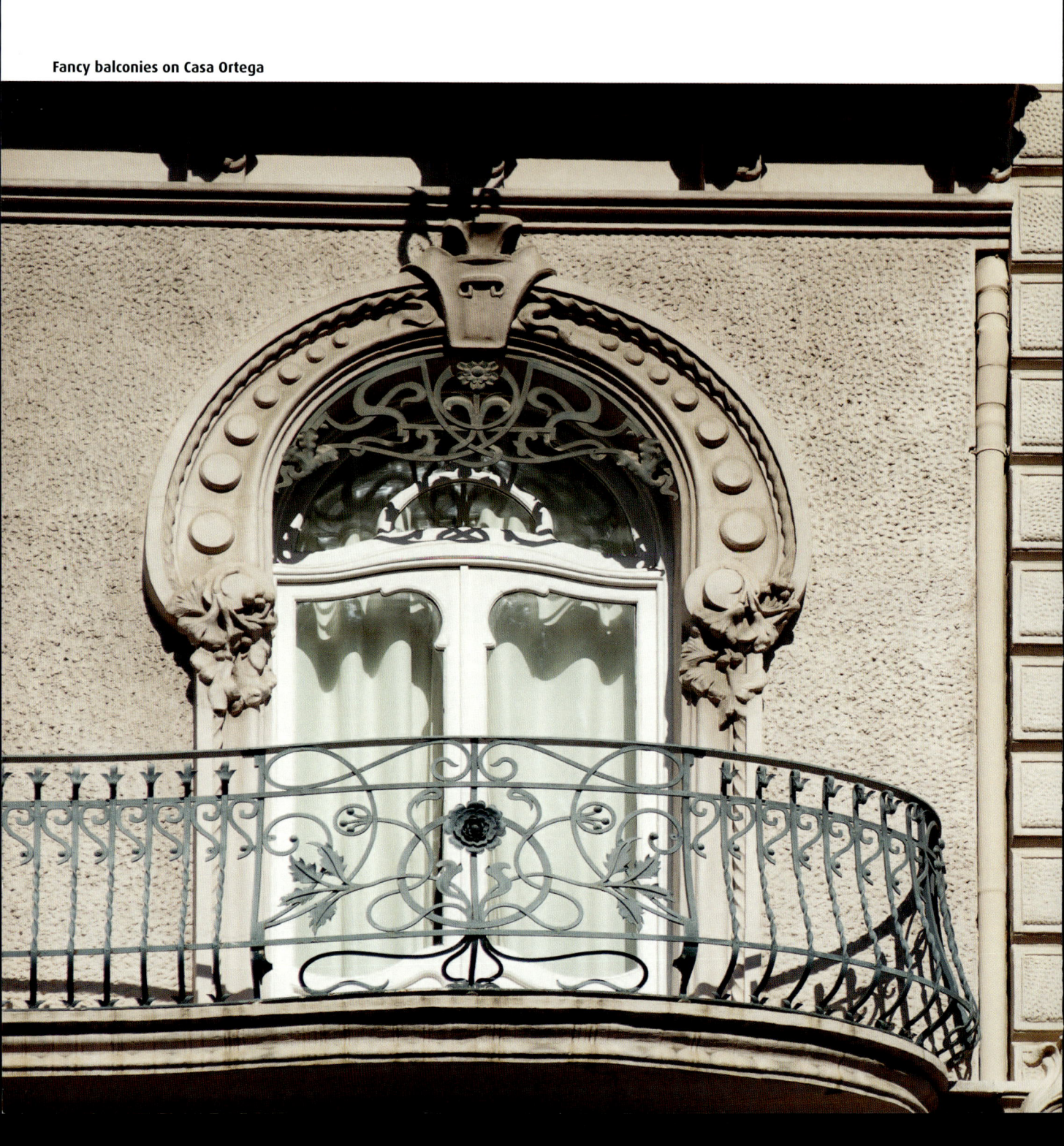

Fancy balconies on Casa Ortega

L'Eixample

By mid-19th century, Valencia was a large city with a population of 100,000 that needed to grow beyond its medieval ramparts. Governor Ciril Amorós began to tear down the city walls in 1865 as an employment scheme. In 1887, the City Council also planned a new urban area according to a project by Joaquín María Arnau, José Calvo and Lluís Ferreres. Thus was born L'Eixample (the Expansion District), partially following the model Ildefons Cerdà applied in Barcelona. The new street grid, as opposed to Barcelona's Eixample, sought to meld with the urban design of the Medieval city. The city wall perimeter became a small, inner-city ring road (ronda).

L'Eixample

Mercat de Colom
(Columbus Market Hall)

Between Carrer de Colom, the Túria Gardens, the train station and Avinguda Peris Valero, the streets were planned in a regular grid pattern, with city blocks having a chamfered square layout, i.e. octagonal blocks, forming small plazas at the chamfered street corners. The housing built here was of high quality, with architects and artists working on buildings that today comprise the most extensive *Modernista* and Eclectic catalogue in the city.

The Columbus Market Hall (Mercat de Colom) is the Eixample's crowning glory. In contrast to the Modernista Central Market Hall in the Old City, which continues its original function, the Colom Market has become a popular leisure area. Built beginning in 1913 by architect Francesc Mora, disciple of Lluís Domènech i Montaner, it has exquisite decorative Valencian ceramic elements.

The Valencian bourgeoisie who were spearheading the turn of the 20th century changes followed the cultural novelties gestating in European society. *Modernisme* or its European counterparts Art Nouveau, Jugendstil, Sezession, Liberty, Modern Style, etc., understood as a free and modern art inspired by nature and the Industrial Revolution, found the appropriate breeding ground in the Valencian artisan tradition (stained glass, woodworking, ceramics, ironwork, etc.) and Fin-de-Siècle fine arts to lend new uses to designs and industrial products in architecture and urban planning.

Valencian *Modernisme*

The personality of Valencians, concerned with taking care of themselves and keeping an impeccable appearance, found the *Modernista* movement a great opportunity to dress the new public and private buildings of the big city in the daring designs and industrial materials that Art Nouveau brought to the bourgeois taste at the turn of the 20th century.

Decades earlier, since the disappearance of the ramparts enclosing the Old City, architectural Eclecticism, with

Columbus Market Hall façade

Noguera II Building

← Inside Columbus Market Hall

L'Eixample

Neoclassical and Mudejar influences, marked the style of the remarkable housing that was being put up in the expansion area. But the arrival of the new style, primarily from Catalonia, turned the development of the modern city into an opportunity to revise the artisan traditions of Valencia and an artistic turning point for their social application using the new industrial codes. Smiths, carpenters, cabinetmakers, sculptors, glass manufacturers, ceramists, etc. placed themselves at the service of architecture to collaborate in the construction of both public and private buildings.

The Eixample or area of expansion was the zone where the most *Modernista* projects were built. The upper middle classes had taken the risk of aesthetic innovation. From this urban area, its influence spread to the other side of the River Túria and the area of port expansion and surrounding neighbourhoods. Other opportunities arose to pay tribute to Modernisme when a major area was cleared in the Old City as a space for the city's large, modern market hall and an avenue into the Old City.

The public and private buildings of Valencian Modernisme, constructed in that period of economic splendour arising from the orange and iron and steel industries, are signed by a remarkable generation of architects. The most renowned are: Francesc Mora (1875-1961), Demetri Ribes (1875-1921), Manuel Peris Ferrando (1872-1934), Josep Manuel Cortina (1868-1950), Xavier Goerlich (1886-1972) and Vicente Ferrer Pérez (1874-1960). Mora applied in Valencia what he had learned at the workshops of outstanding Catalan architects such as Gaudí and Domènech i Montaner, and in his years as a student in Barcelona. Ribes was trained in Madrid and was a great connoisseur of the Viennese architecture of Otto Wagner. Ferrer was remarkable as a master in the application of the so-called 'minor' or decorative arts. Goerlich, son of the Austrian consul, was the municipal architect for several decades.

Casa Sánchez de León, former Illa de Cuba department store

Casa del Punt del Ganxo

L'Eixample

Estació del Nord
(North Station)

Built from 1906 to 1917 by Demetri Ribes very close to City Hall so that train passengers could arrive directly in the heart of the city, its precious lobby is a brilliant expression of Mediterranean vitality on a Modernista note. Valencian women in traditional country garb, exuberant orange trees, the typical *barraca* mudbrick houses of the wetlands, fishing scenes in L'Albufera lagoon, ironwork – the lobby's ornamental motifs reflect Valencia's social and economic boom during the years the station was being built.

This place, today complemented by the AVE Station, covers the history of the railway from the steam engine to the high-speed train. When the old station was inaugurated, it was designed to offer travellers a dazzling image of the land where they were arriving. And Modernisme provided a brilliant architectural setting. The main focus was on the values and traditions of Valencian identity, offering an image of a rich, fertile land.

Upon leaving the station, visitors encounter some of the most elegant buildings in the city, scattered from there to the Plaça de l'Ajuntament (Town Hall Square).

Plaça de Bous
(Bullring)

Designed by Sebastià Monleón and located just next to the train station (Estació del Nord), it was built between 1850 and 1860 following the Neoclassical lines of a Roman coliseum. A perfectly round structure with four floors, it has 384 symmetrical arches. Spain's bullfighting season begins in Valencia in March, during the Falles festival. The Bullfighting Museum next to the bullring commemorates the greatest triumphs achieved in the arena.

North Station ticket office

Station lobby

← Above: North Station
Below: Bullring

Shopping and Leisure Route

Valencia is a city renowned for its tradition of commerce. It is a leading market in the export of agricultural produce. The Sant Francesc and Eixample neighbourhoods, in the area around the Colom Market, have consolidated a top-notch shopping area, with department stores and shops offering the world's leading brands. In the area, Poeta Querol Street is a small island dubbed 'the Golden Mile', with some of the most exclusive brand names of European fashion.

Hand-crafted products are sold next to new consumer products, youth and adult fashion, fresh design, new technology and the latest in sophisticated trends. The best clothing and household product designers have shops on both sides of Carrer de Colom. The avalanche of shops, reinforced by the many company offices setting up here, has not prevented the bourgeois population from continuing to occupy their homes in the splendid flats built when the Eixample was designed.

In Valencia, fashion can be bought at a great variety of prices, at department stores or small shops, because the offer ranges from leading fashion firms and boutiques showcasing emerging designers to local brand-name shops. Valencian designers are experts at working with leather, knitwear, silk and natural fibres. The abundance of quality shoe and handbag shops will satisfy any taste. Another high point is the latest design in home products and household linen, and shops with trendy designer objects.

This is a good place to buy souvenirs of your trip. Ceramics and other handcrafted goods are distinguished elements of the city's tradition. There are also food shops — true emporia of taste and aroma. Book, photography and music shops offer an endless range of articles as well.

Carrer de Colom

Shop on Carrer Císcar

Russafa

This former outlying agricultural town was annexed to the city of Valencia in 1877. Towards the 9th century, a Moorish farmstead was built in the south with a large green area two kilometres from the walled Balansiya. The natural beauty of the park and irrigation channels were sung by poets of the time, and hence the area's name, after the Arabic word *rusafat*, in reference to the famous gardens in ancient Syria.

Russafa inhabitants specialised in floating logs felled from the forests of Els Serrans down the River Túria to the port, with the help of poles with large hooks. The town was dubbed *terra del ganxo* (hook-land).

When 20th-century urban planning was done here, the irregular street layout of this town was fused with the chamfered square block planning of Valencia's Eixample, creating a harmonious combination between two very different urban design concepts. Today Russafa is also part of District 2, i.e. the (extended) Eixample.

At present, it has an intense intercultural life due to the high ratio of immigrants and artists and designers with studios in the area. Modern art spaces can be found together with elements displaying the newcomers' cultures of origin, reproducing the open, young atmosphere generated in El Carme in the 1970s.

Graffiti

Russafa - a creative, open-minded place

↑ **Russafa Market Hall** ↓ **Street/commercial art**

Església de Sant Valeri
(Saint Valerius Church)

This is the most emblematic building in the neighbourhood. It was built over the ruins of an older church that burnt down in 1415. The architecture was by Master Tomàs Lleonard Esteve and the Baroque ornamentation by Juan Bautista Pérez Castiel.

Mercat de Russafa
(Russafa Market Hall)

The neighbourhood's intense activity can be discovered every morning at the market, where tastes and products of different cultures coexist. It was built by the Town Council in 1957, during the Franco period, to improve social conditions in the area. The austere lines of the building are livened by the colours of its façades. Nearby is the Monastery of Our Lady of the Angels (Convent de la Mare de Déu dels Àngels), where James I of Aragon signed the capitulations of the Moorish king of Balansiya.

Cupolas of Saint Valerius Church

Market stall

Sala Russafa
(Russafa Hall)

This cultural venue is the result of refurbishing a former industrial machinery factory located at Carrer de Dénia 55. An auditorium that seats 174, two rehearsal spaces and an exhibit and conference hall is the project set up by the theatre company Arden Producciones.

Sala Russafa

Túria Gardens
A river without water, given over to leisure and culture

Afternoon-evening swing dancing under Calatrava's Exposició Bridge

Túria Gardens

On 14 October 1957, the River Túria caused its last, tragic flood of Valencia, with a death toll of 81 and major material damage. The City Council decided to end the regular flooding by rerouting the river to flow around the city, funding the initiative through a special 25-cent stamp that was obligatory for any letters leaving the city for many years. Twelve kilometres of riverbed were thus freed up for other urban uses. Pressure from the inhabitants in 1980 led to the planting of the first trees of what is now the city's most extensive green area and sports zone, stopping attempts to convert the strip into a motorway.

↑ **Pond at Parc de la Capçalera** ↓ **Elephants at the Bioparc**

Parc de la Capçalera

Architects Arancha Muñoz, Eduardo de Miguel and Vicente Corell were commissioned to devise a tribute to the presence of water in the city, in the uppermost section of the recently drained Túria river course. The park is designed like an *assut*, a water flow regulator or technique for channelling water whose design dates back to Moorish times, distributed in several large platforms. It lies at the point where the Túria Gardens meet the last part of the river before it is diverted towards the Plan Sud, i.e. the river's new path. A lookout point allows a view of the entire area: the pond with its paddleboats and islands, walking paths and groves of trees.

Bioparc

The Bioparc is a modern zoo offering cutting-edge, ample infrastructures to make the animals feel at home and allow the public to enjoy viewing them. In this new zoo, which substitutes the conventional one formerly in the Jardins de Vivers or del Real, there are no cages. The animals can be observed from a distance as they tranquilly go about their lives. In a surface area of 10 thousand square metres, different African ecosystems are reproduced.

Museu d'Història de València

The Catalan engineer and architect Ildefons Cerdà built this beautiful underground water reservoir in 1850, today restructured as a museum. The 2,200 years of the city's history are shown in these facilities with the aid of new technologies, confirming that the former River Túria has become a 'river of culture', since institutions of great interest are now located on both riverbanks. The museum is next to the border with the neighbouring town of Mislata.

A great place for sports

The Túria Gardens are a sanctuary for athletes and cyclists, a meeting point for practicing any sport and participating in exercise and physical culture movements. La Petxina Sports Complex, located in a revamped former abattoir built in 1898 on the right bank, offers housing and facilities for elite athletes.

Hypostyle or pillared hall, Valencian History Museum

Túria Gardens, an ideal place for sport

↑ **Pont del Real** ↓ **Pont dels Serrans**

Túria Gardens

The bridges

The creation of the Túria Gardens, a nearly one-million-square-metre park open 24 hours a day that's easily accessible from any neighbourhood, represents the main urban renovation carried out in Valencia in the past few decades. Three sections of note are: the one designed by architect Ricardo Bofill, near the Palau de la Música concert hall, with a neoclassical air; Parc Gulliver, designed especially for children by the Falles artist Manolo Martín, the illustrator Sento Llobell and the architect Rafael Rivera; and the Ciutat de les Arts i les Ciències (City of Arts and Sciences).

The Túria riverbed is crossed by 20 bridges, half of them built after 1960. The following are a selection of the most interesting. Pont de la Mar, which has been pedestrian since 1933, is the most artistic of the old bridges. Pont d'Aragó, an extension of Gran Via del Marqués del Túria, is an essential connection to the Poblats Marítims area along the coast and port zone. Pont del Regne de València is also known as Pont dels Dimonis (Demon Bridge) for the four winged creatures like fallen angels guarding its two ends. The Pont de l'Àngel Custodi (Guardian Angel Bridge) was built in 1949; the Pont de l'Exposició was erected by Santiago Calatrava over a metro station; the Pont de les Flors has sidewalks and planters with geraniums; and the Pont del 9 d'Octubre, from 1989, was the first architectural piece Calatrava built in his native city.

Pont del Mar

Demon on Pont del Regne de València

Calatrava's Pont de l'Exposició

Túria Gardens

Museu de Belles Arts
(Museum of Fine Arts)

This Baroque-style building was originally designed in the early 18th century to house seminarians, but was later turned into a military hospital and warehouse. In 1925, the church lost its roof, which caved in due to disrepair, but it has since been rebuilt. It was not until the 1940s that it began to house a significant classical art collection that had previously been on deposit at the Carme Monastery. The Renaissance courtyard of the Palace of Ambassador Vich was transferred to the museum some years ago, intended as a new entrance from the Jardins del Real gardens.

The most important part of the collection consists of the Gothic panels by the Valencian Primitive School, which made artworks of great value during the city's apogee in the 14th and 15th centuries. These works were by painters the likes of Jacomart, Pere Nicolau, Joan Reixach and Nicolau Falcó, as well as the sculptor Damià Forment. The other important part of the collection is that of the Masters of Great Valencian Art, from the late 19th and turn of the 20th century, with painter Joaquim Sorolla leading this generation, together with the painters and sculptors Ignasi Pinazo, Josep Benlliure, Antonio Muñoz Degrain, Francesc Domingo Marqués, Joaquim Agrasot, etc. European painting is represented by El Greco, Hieronymus Bosch and Van Dyck, not to mention portraits by Goya and Academic works by José de Madrazo and Vicent López, as well as the highly-regarded Velázquez, Murillo and Zurbarán.

Palace of Ambassador Vich, courtyard

← **Altarpieces in the Fine Arts Museum**

Sorolla Room

Jardins del Real
(Royal Palace Gardens)

Centuries ago, this urban garden was the park of the Royal Palace, residence of the Valencian monarchs. The archaeological remains of the palace lie under Carrer del General Elio and at the garden entrance. Some of the more renowned areas in the Gardens are the stage where the July Fair concerts take place and the promenade where the annual book fair is held. In the right-hand area of the entrance across from the river, visitors can stroll through an intricate labyrinth of Neoclassical gazebos and parterres. The latest expansion of the gardens took place in 1974, with the addition of a rose garden and a cypress-lined avenue with a sculpture by the acclaimed Andreu Alfaro.

The enclosure around the park is from the Parterre, a garden in la Xerea created by the French. The history of this green area begins with the Moorish king known as Ali Bufat Mulei (Ali Abu Fadl), who built a leisure home outside the city walls.

Royal Palace Gardens

Museu de Ciències Naturals
(Natural Science Museum)

Located in the Jardins del Real, in a former restaurant, this building has been remodelled to provide space for notable scientific exhibits. The permanent exhibit contains Josep Rodrigo Botet's Quaternary palaeontology collection from South America, as well as the contributions of the scientists Eduard Boscà Casanoves, Antoni Cabanilles and Santiago Ramón y Cajal during their Valencian period, among other things.

Jardí de Joaquín Monforte Parrés (Monforte Garden)

Juan Bautista Romero, marquis of San Juan, decided to build a small palace with a romantic garden in 1849, in an area filled with horticultural gardens and aristocratic villas. The works were commissioned to the architect Sebastià Monleón Estellés. The two lions sculpted by José Bellver embellishing the garden were intended to stand before the doors of the Congress of Deputies in Madrid, but the honourable MPs rejected them for being too small.

Natural Science Museum

Monforte Garden →

Túria Gardens

Passeig de l'Albereda
(Albereda Promenade)

Recreational area on the other side of the river which, after the city walls were torn down, became a favourite area for the nobility and bourgeoisie to show off their carriages in the late 19th century. Beginning in 1871, this was where the festive pavilions of the July Fair were set up, and where the ornate parade of the Battle of the Flowers was held. The first poplars planted in the mid-17th century gave the promenade its name.

Palau de l'Exposició
(Exposition Palace)

The architect Francesc Mora built this example of traditional Valencian architecture revised by Modernisme during the glory years Valencia experienced when it held the Regional and National Expositions of 1909 and 1910, respectively. Next to the Palace, the Casa de Lactància (a nursing ward for the babies of working mothers) also dates from this period.

Palau de la Música
(Concert Hall)

This concert hall is the city's main auditorium, although the opera house is nearby. Built in 1984 by architect José María García de Paredes, its main auditorium has impeccable acoustics. The façade consists of a lovely glass vault evoking the crystal palaces of the 19th century. From the terrace, you can see the gardens designed by Ricardo Bofill. The pool has a fountain programmed for music and light shows. This is the official headquarters of the Valencia Orchestra. In its different halls and auditoriums, the building can seat over 2,100 spectators.

← Above: Passeig de l'Albereda
Below: Palau de la Música concert hall

Ferris Wheel in the Túria Gardens opposite L'Albereda

The turn-of-the-century Exposition Palace

City of Arts and Sciences
A new urban image

City of Arts and Sciences

This major architectural project is part of a city renovation scheme, creating a new focal point and pole of tourist attraction at the former mouth of the River Túria. At the same time, the former industrial area has been turned into a neighbourhood of modern residential blocks. Its surface area of 350,000 square metres, the largest urban complex for cultural, educational and recreational ends built in Europe in the past few years, is an emblem of 21st-century Valencia. The complex is home to art, science and nature in advanced-technology infrastructures.

City of Arts and Sciences

Palau de les Arts

The Palace of the Arts opera house was built in 2005 at the top vertex of the cultural complex. At first the location was to be occupied by a communications tower, but this was revised because of the air traffic corridor passing through here. Two rolled steel shells make up the building's outer skin. Its four spaces offer a notable opera, symphonic music and ballet season.

The use of white concrete in all the buildings of the Ciutat complex and the presence of thin sheets of water distributed in immense pools are effects intentionally sought by the architect Santiago Calatrava to capture the Mediterranean light and reflect a certain nostalgia for the former river. In this futuristic-looking site in Valencia, Calatrava has brought together all manners and styles of construction that have made him famous the world over.

L'Hemisfèric

Inaugurated in 1998, this IMAX cinema can seat 300 people. The building represents a large-scale human eye gazing placidly over a pool of water. The eyelid with lashes can open and close thanks to an intelligent hydraulic engineering project.

It was the first building to go up in this entertainment megacity. The project was only going to include a large science museum, but when the works definitively got underway, the performing arts cultural elements and the aquarium were added.

Two years after the IMAX cinema was inaugurated, the science museum opened. In 2002 the Oceanogràfic opened, becoming the most visited facility of the entire complex. And finally, in 2005, the curtain was raised at the opera house.

Palau de les Arts opera house

L'Hemisfèric, IMAX cinema and planetarium, with its "eye" open

City of Arts and Sciences

Museu de les Ciències (Science Museum)

Over 42,000 square meters distributed on five levels were created by the architect Calatrava to display new and old science, with exhibits that make the use of scientific discoveries easy for anyone to understand. The outer arches, over 40 metres high, represent the spinal column of an imaginary diplodocus, turning the monumentality of this building into something unreal, a futuristic image. The large water pools around it, in which the audacious architectural forms are reflected, accentuate the fantasy of the setting. In just a few years, this atmosphere has made the Ciutat become an effective commercial platform for advertisements, film shoots and social and corporate events. The architect has applied visual unity to the project, as established, for instance, through the use of the Modernista-style *trencadís* (broken ceramic tile surfacing) in blue and white tones, which seek the results that Gaudí so brilliantly achieved in Barcelona.

Science Museum

L'Umbracle

This shade house is a symbolic entrance to the major entertainment complex. It is a 7000-square-metre green area covered by a metallic, trellis-like structure adorned with vegetation and livened by sculptures by Yoko Ono, Miquel Navarro and other artists. It also serves as a botanical garden that is home to 50 native species, among other Mediterranean plants. Under it is a spacious car park for visitors to the Ciutat.

The Umbracle and Àgora were designed to complement the four most significant projects comprising the mainstay of the architectural complex — the Palau de les Arts (opera house), the Museu de les Ciències (science museum), the Hemisfèric (IMAX), and the Oceanogràfic (oceanarium).

L'Umbracle shade house

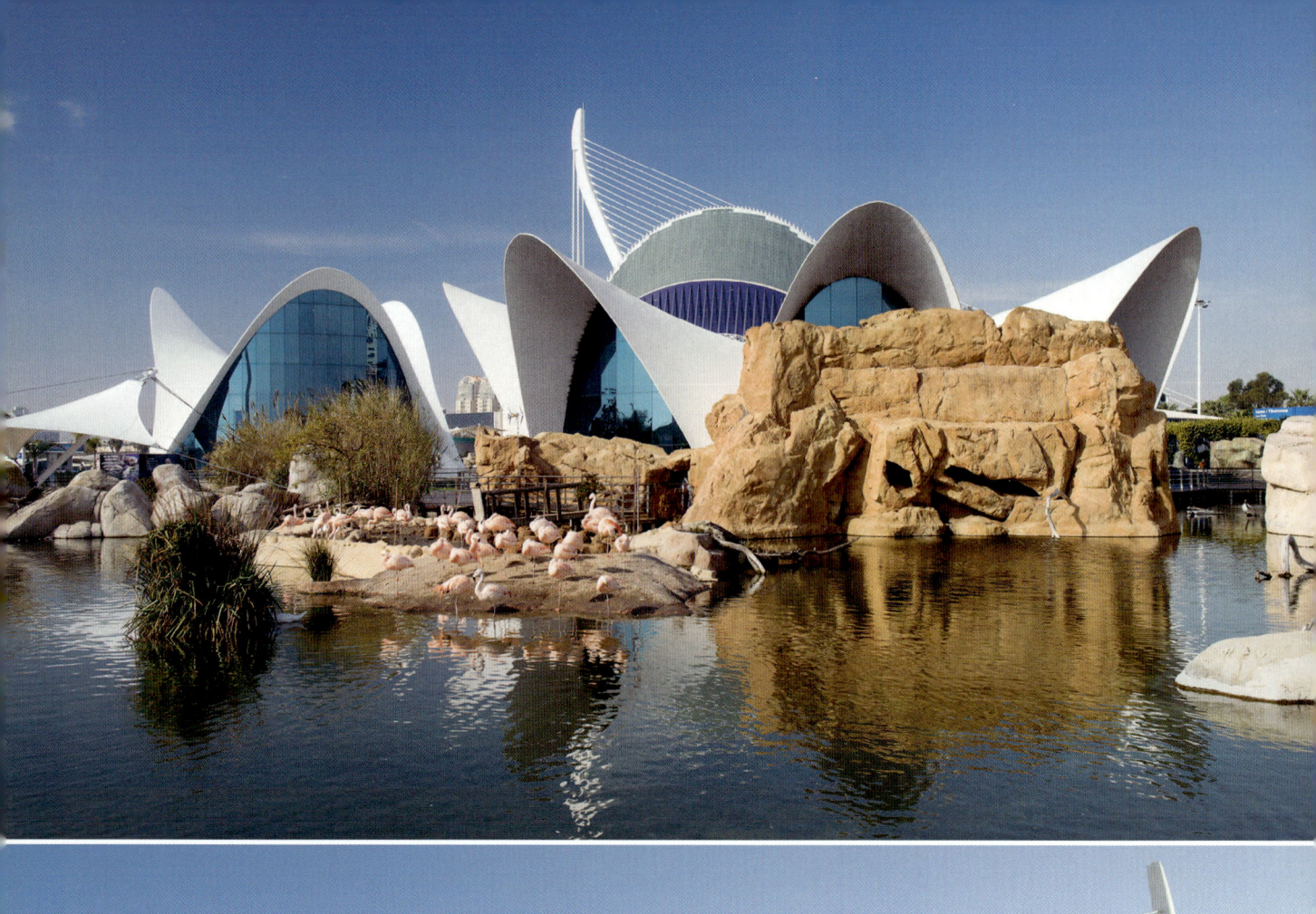

City of Arts and Sciences

L'Oceanogràfic

This submerged city is considered the largest aquarium in Europe. Created by architect Félix Candela with the collaboration of Adrián López and the engineers Alberto Domingo and Carlos Lázaro, it is populated by over 45,000 aquatic animals, including birds, living in recreations of their natural habitats. There are ten areas allowing visitors to see the different marine ecosystems of the world in a relatively short time span.

Each building is associated with the aquatic environments of the Mediterranean, temperate and tropical seas, wetlands, oceans, the Arctic, the Antarctic and islands. Red Sea species can be found in a large aquarium that serves as a backdrop to the auditorium stage. One of the major attractions are the dolphin shows, at an open-air dolphinarium measuring 10.5 square metres and holding 24 million litres of water.

L'Àgora

This multiple-use building was inaugurated in 2010 with an Open Tennis Tournament, but is also intended for social and official events. It is designed to resemble a large public square, but protected by a 70-metre-high roof. One of the more striking elements of this huge building is the cobalt blue *trencadís* (broken ceramic tile surfacing), whose colour alludes to the cupolas of Valencian churches.

Pont de l'Assut de l'Or
(Assut de l'Or Bridge)

This bridge is 180 metres long and 125 metres high. A large tower or pylon supports the structure with cable stays. It is named after the *assut*, the mechanism that used to regulate the river's water flow as a sort of weir. The strong pylon is one of the tallest and most emblematic structures in the Ciutat de les Arts i les Ciències complex. It connects Valencia's Bulevar Sud with the continuation of the city's fourth ring road.

← Above: L'Oceanogràfic complex
  Below: L'Àgora and Assut de l'Or Bridge

Ocean tank tunnel at the Oceanogràfic

Calatrava's Assut de l'Or Bridge

The Port, El Cabanyal and the Beaches

The most Mediterranean Valencia

The Port, El Cabanyal and the Beaches

When they say Valencia lives with its back to the sea, it's probably a reference to the time when the seafront was occupied by Poble Nou del Mar, an independent agricultural and fishing town where the city's upper classes went to spend the summer when the fashion of taking sea baths began. This seafront area was administratively joined to the capital in 1897, but it maintained a large part of its customs. Now there is no longer a social distance between the historic centre of Valencia and the seafront neighbourhoods due to the major commercial expansion of the port and the development of the area as the city's beach and seafront promenade.

↑ **Edifici del Rellotge (Clock Tower Building)**   ↓ **One of the Modernista Tinglado warehouses**

TINGLADO Nº 2

The Port, El Cabanyal and the Beaches

Marina Real Juan Carlos I

In the 2010s, the city rediscovered its seafront after profoundly transforming the port to turn it into a modern marina in time for the international America's Cup sailing competition and the provisional construction of a Formula 1 racetrack.

The shift of Valencia's downtown area towards the east as an effect of the construction of the Ciutat de les Arts i les Ciències and the organisation of these international sports events have generated a new social impulse and pole of tourist attraction in the maritime neighbourhoods. The Marina Juan Carlos I occupies the oldest part of the port, around the elegant Edifici del Rellotge (a building named after its clock tower).

The new breakwater and wharves have become a space admired by nautical sports lovers in the Mediterranean. The redevelopment has also allowed for extra moorings, greater dock space for cruise ships and provision of services for programming sports and social events.

There are three Modernista buildings in the marina: the Tinglados (warehouses), the Varador Públic (boathouse) built in red brick, and the Docks Comercials building, a former warehouse in brick now hosting evening entertainment.

Relaxed atmosphere near the Clock Tower Building

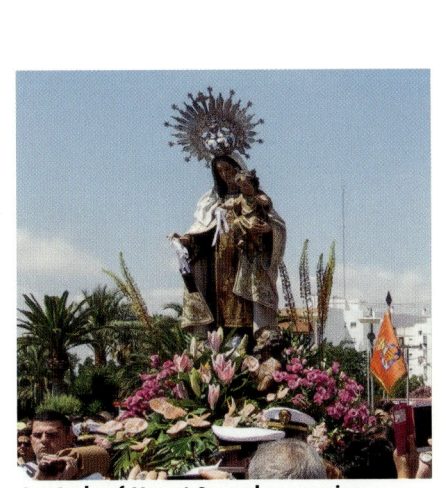

Our Lady of Mount Carmel procession

Daybreak at the Juan Carlos I Marina

Les Drassanes (Shipyards)

This Gothic building was put up in the 14th century next to the church of Santa Maria del Mar and sports a wooden roof and gates allowing the entrance and exit of ships, which is no longer possible since there are now tall buildings where the water once was. After it expropriated the facilities in 1980, the City Council has occupied them with interesting temporary exhibits and a maritime museum.

Veles e Vents Building

The work of architect David Chipperfield, in collaboration with the Fermín Vázquez Studio, it is an artistic statement and an emblem of the new port. Its image is directly associated with the America's Cup competition. The building is on a new wharf that houses bars and restaurants and next to the new canal that boats used to access the marine competition area. It consists of four immense platforms that are staggered to create areas of shade.

Inside the Gothic shipyards

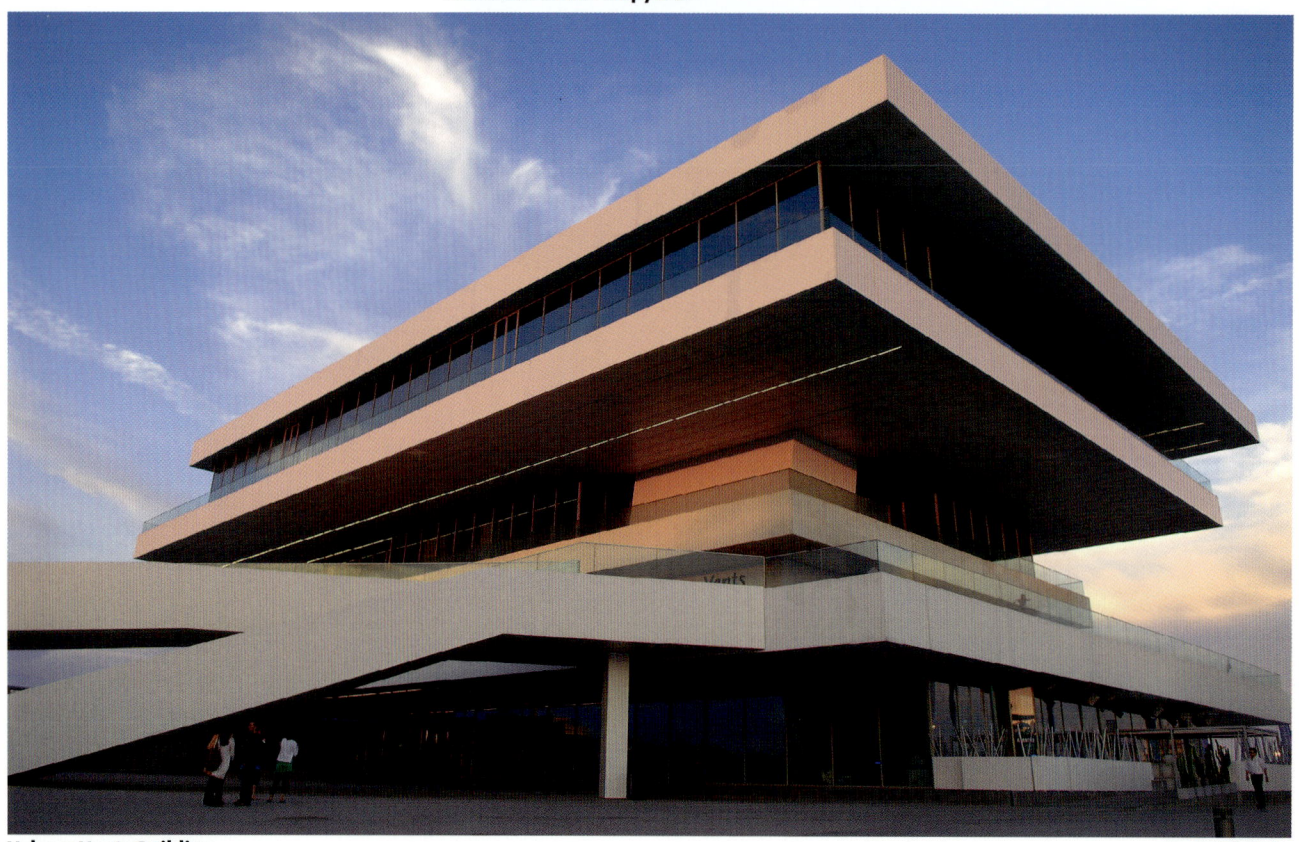

Veles e Vents Building

Casa Calabuig →

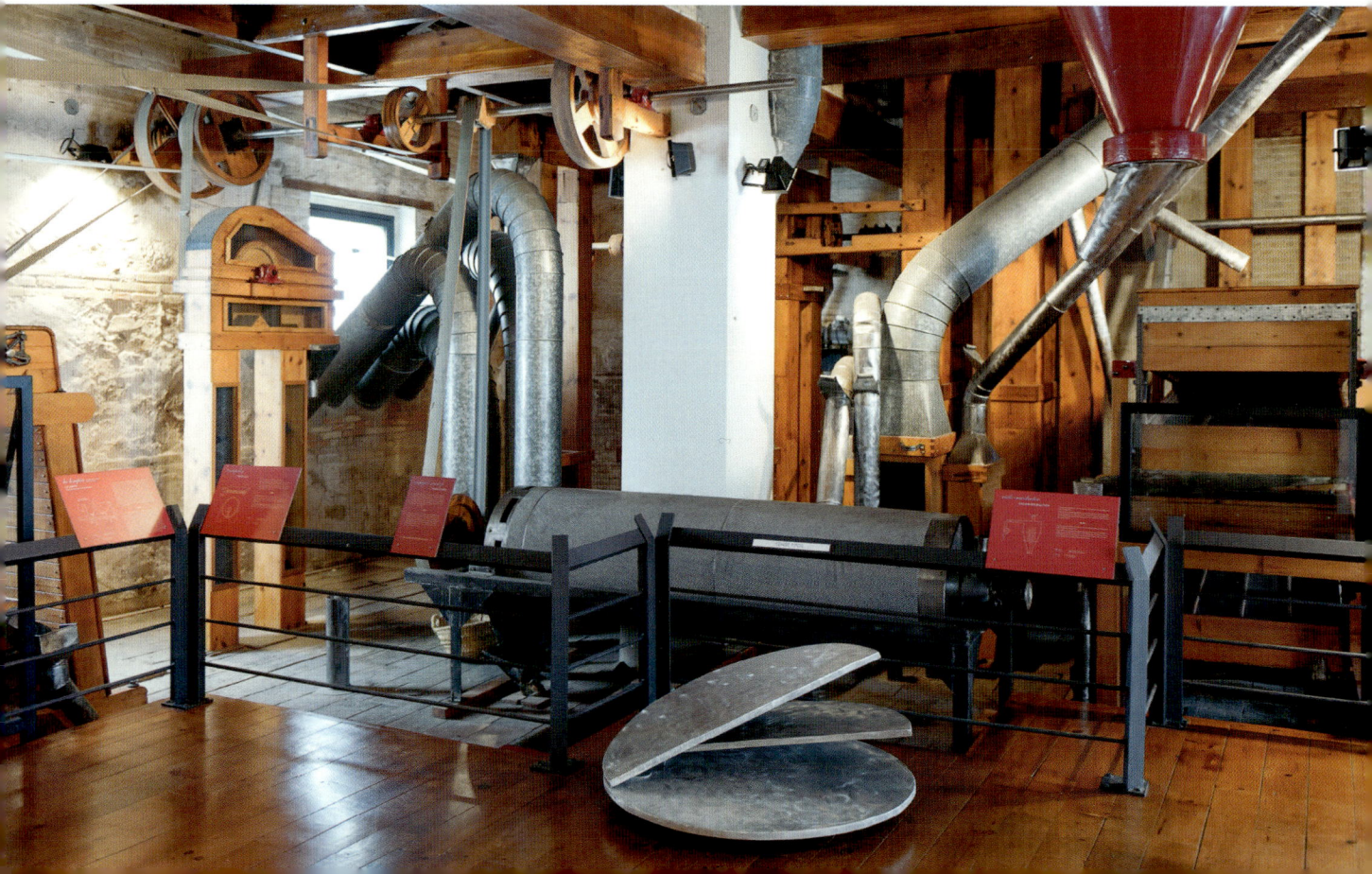

↑ El Cabanyal's lovely colours ↓ Rice Museum

The Port, El Cabanyal and the Beaches

El Cabanyal

The Poblats Marítims is a district grouping together five historic neighbourhoods. The first one, Natzaret, in the south, became isolated from the sea when it lost its beach due to the redevelopment of the port. The second is El Grau (which means port), located at the entrance to the port. After that come the areas of El Cabanyal and Canyamelar, with their long streets. And finally, La Malva-rosa, the northernmost seafront neighbourhood.

Lately, due to the popularity of the grass-roots movement, *Salvem el Cabanyal* (Let's Save El Cabanyal), against the extension of Avinguda Blasco Ibáñez to the sea because it would break the neighbourhood's traditional layout, the entire seafront area is often simply called El Cabanyal. In the end, the voice of the people won out over the political wishes of the previous, majority-conservative City Council Administration.

The streets are remarkable for their ornamental houses in Modernista style. The brick smokestacks belong to former factories, some of them making alcoholic beverages. The Marine Holy Week Museum (Museu de la Setmana Santa Marinera), dedicated to one of the neighbourhood's longest-standing traditions, is housed in a former rice mill dating back to 1902. The Church of Our Lady of the Rosary (from 1845) is a focal point of this festival. Before its latest reform, El Musical, a theatre in the heart of El Cabanyal, was home to the Ateneu Musical del Port, the port area's symphony orchestra.

Vernacular Modernisme in El Cabanyal

Paella

El Musical Theatre

Platja de les Arenes

The city's first beach resort was opened here in 1888, where there is now a modern, luxury hotel with views to the sea from every room. Two pavilions in Classical Greek style still remain standing from the original spa, where they served as separate men's and women's changing rooms.

The architect Luis Gutiérrez Soto built two pools at the spa in the 1930s, one exclusively for children, applying construction designs from naval architecture to the trampoline tower and the café-bar area.

↑ **Arenes beach**   ↓ **Hotel Balneario Las Arenas resort**

The Port, El Cabanyal and the Beaches

Platja de la Malva-rosa

Malva-rosa is the best-known section of this long sandy beach because the painter Joaquim Sorolla and the writer Vicente Blasco Ibáñez popularised it in their works. The former painted bathers and fishermen and the latter wrote novels from the balcony of his chalet, now a museum. At the seafront are the houses where the Valencian upper middle class spent their summer holidays.

Just in front of them is a long, wide seafront promenade full of palm trees, making this one of the most attractive and comfortable beaches on the Mediterranean. There is a wide range of restaurants offering paella and seafood overlooking the sea.

Blasco Ibáñez House Museum

City of the Future
21st Century Valencia

Norman Foster's Palau de Congressos (Congress Centre)

City of the Future

Valencia is planning its future in four interrelated areas: trade and commerce, tourism, scientific innovation and corporate renewal. The upgrading of the trade fair and exhibitions centre coincides with the significant increase in port activity and the rise in business and conventions tourism. At the university, innovation takes priority, and there are also different biomedical research facilities in different places in the city. The increased arrival of cruise ships and the new orientation towards sporting events have also made tourism a resource for growth.

↑ **Telecommunications Engineering School, UPV**   ↓ **Valencia University (UV) Language Centre**

City of the Future

Tarongers University Campus

When two university campuses were inaugurated — the Polytechnic University's science campus and the University of Valencia's humanities campus (the former dating from the 1970s with new elements, the latter completely new) — on Avinguda dels Tarongers (Orange Tree Avenue), the city opened up another path to the sea in parallel to Avinguda de Blasco Ibáñez. After the area of schools and faculties, the Ciutat Politècnica de la Innovació (Polytechnic City of Innovation) was built, an architectural reflection of a new era in teaching and research. The project by architect Luis Manuel Ferrer Obanos has allowed the construction of a polyvalent building for changing uses made of new materials created through modern technology.

Avinguda de les Corts Valencianes

This is one of the town's most modern thoroughfares, which extends the city north-westwards with the construction of high-rises providing office and business space as well as housing. The construction of Valencia's new football stadium, and the opening of various large hotels and many bars and restaurants have consolidated the leisure, tourism and urban uses that began with the inauguration of the Palau de Congressos (Congress Centre) in 1993, which served as a revitalising element close to the Palau de Fires (Trade Fair Centre) designed to foster a new focal point in the city's northwest corner.

Valencia University (UV) Law Faculty

Dama Ibèrica (Iberian Lady), by Manolo Valdés

Universitat Politècnica de València (UPV) – Valencia Tech

↑ Congress Centre ↓ Valencia Trade Fair Auditorium

City of the Future

Palau de Congressos
(Congress Centre)

Norman Foster's project constitutes an architectural icon for this part of Valencia, its enormous roof standing out amid the fields and horticultural plots still existing in the neighbourhood at the time of its inauguration. Today, the tall buildings all along the avenue minimize the effect sought by the ingenious Foster. Its very horizontal layout does not prevent it from gathering the great light and warmth of the Mediterranean through its immense windows. Around it is an extensive rose garden and ponds with fountains. Some fifty congresses a year take place in its modern halls.

Fira de València
Palau de Fira de Mostres de Benimàmet
(Valencia Trade Fair Centre)

The Fira de València, the city's trade fair institution, was pioneering when it was created in 1917 to foster the economy's export capacity. The constant expansion and modernisation of its facilities in the neighbourhood of Benimàmet has had its latest expression in the inauguration of a modern Events Centre, rounding off the complex's numerous pavilions, recently unified through the overarching reform done by architect José María Tomás Llavador. Over the course of the year, some forty trade fairs take place here, the furniture and ceramics fairs being the busiest. Some hundred monographic exhibitions and events complete the business offer at this Valencian venue.

EDEM Escuela de Empresarios
(EDEM Business School)

What was once the nautical sports teams' headquarters is now a business school and a seed fund and start-up accelerator for entrepreneurial projects. The school, located in the Port Marina area and forming part of the university network, is backed by Valencian businesspeople.

Circuit Ricardo Tormo
(Ricardo Tormo Motorsport Racetrack)

With an infrastructure appropriate for automobile and motorcycle competitions, this race track bears the name of the famous Valencian Grand Prix motorcycle road racer who was two-time world champion in the 50-cc category. Located 26 kilometres from Valencia in the town of Xest, it can hold 120,000 spectators (seating 60,000). The mild climate allows numerous European winter races.

EDEM

L'Albufera and L'Horta
Valencia's Farming & Fishing Belt

L'Albufera Natural Park

L'Albufera and L'Horta

The geological plains forming on both sides of the River Túria, together with the abundance of groundwater feeding wells and fountains, have turned the coastal landscape of Valencia into an immense garden ready to supply household shopping carts and the area's rich gastronomy. The area around L'Albufera (a coastal lagoon south of the city centre) and the historic area of L'Horta "The Garden", a market garden expanse around Valencia) maintain their agricultural identity despite urban growth and the creation of new industrial estates. The former area is dedicated to rice monoculture, while in the latter, a patchwork of horticultural plots supply fresh produce to the city's marketplaces.

L'Albufera and L'Horta

Parc Natural de l'Albufera

In its southern reaches, the municipality of Valencia enjoys a natural park where the agricultural tasks of rice cultivation combine with nature and beach tourism.

Over the centuries, it was considered an unhealthy area, with its stagnant water, and was reserved as hunting grounds for the Spanish monarchy. In the 19th century it did not lose its public status, but ownership shifted to the Valencia City Council. Today the park is managed by thirteen town councils, though the Franco Administration attempted to privatize it. The construction of holiday apartments has only affected a sector of the park's beaches.

L'Albufera is a 21,000-hectare wetland area where migrating birds stop, primarily on their way from Northern Europe to Northern Africa and back. The freshwater lagoon, called albufera by the Moors, is actually an inland sea, separated from the Mediterranean by a cordon of dunes and pine groves where visitors love to stroll. The lagoon's contact with the sea is regulated by three channels with sluice gates.

The Albufera fishermen hire out boats to people wishing to navigate the lake and observe its rich flora and fauna. Some maintain the traditional boats propelled by the wind power of the lateen rig or the arm power of the pole, used to push off against the bottom to move the boat forward.

The most attractive moment of a visit to the park is sunset, when the sun paints the sky and the mountains on the horizon a thousand colours.

Albufera Fishermen

Western swamphen (*Porphyrio porphyrio*)

↑ **Dune recovery at El Saler Beach** ↓ **Rice fields after the harvest**

L'Albufera and L'Horta

El Saler
The park's coastal area offers the opportunity to enjoy lovely beaches. The most popular one is El Saler, because it's connected to an urban area with good restaurants and lodgings. Taking a swim is a good follow-up to a morning spent observing nature. The beaches are located on the sandbar that connects the mouths of the Rivers Túria and Xúquer, created by alluvial sediments deposited by the rivers over millennia.

El Palmar
El Palmar is a town that grew up between the waters of the lagoon and the park's channels, whose inhabitants know the Albufera customs of fishing and duck hunting. Its streets offer a plethora of restaurants serving good paella at any time of day, as well as other specialities of Valencian gastronomy such as eels, mussels and a variety of fresh seafood. Before reaching El Palmar, you will come across the park's bird observatory.

The rice fields
The lakeside is dedicated to the cultivation of rice on land won over from the lagoon. A park system for flooding the rice paddies is activated in autumn to allow the rice seedlings to grow. In spring the paddies are drained.

The Valencian *barraca* or adobe hut
Around El Palmar are some examples of these whitewashed mudbrick houses, a traditional construction of the Horta area around Valencia that has presently fallen out of use — they are no longer built nor lived in. They are rectangular buildings with an acute sloping roof that nearly reaches the ground, made of straw and different types of reed, all products growing locally. The walls are made of adobe bricks.

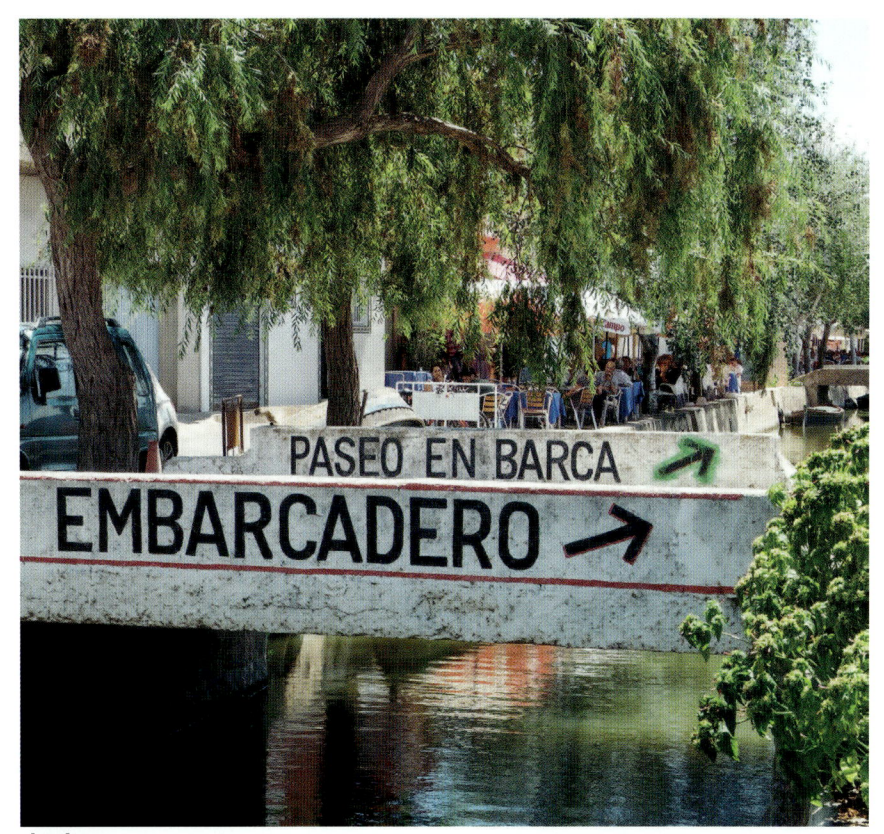

El Palmar

Barraca d'Amparo in El Palmar

L'Albufera and L'Horta

L'Horta de València

The Valencian Horta or horticultural area, the major expanse of market garden plots surrounding the capital, especially to the north and south, hails from the period of Islamic rule. Although the Romans had already introduced the cultivation of grapes, olive trees and cereals in the area, a significant agricultural leap occurred during the seven centuries of Moorish presence, consolidating a major network of irrigation channels and small weirs and diversion channels called assuts that regulated the river's flow and allowed an extensive area of land to be turned into an irrigation farming zone. At that time, horticultural products began to be cultivated, as well as rice, *xufla* or *chufa* (tiger nut), not to mention artichoke and aubergine, with citruses being added to the panoply more recently.

From that period dates the millenarian Tribunal de les Aigües (Water Tribunal), an institution that administers justice off the paper record in conflicts arising in the distribution of water through Valencia's eight major irrigation channels: Montcada, Tormos, Mestalla, Rascanya, Quart, Mislata, Rovella and Favara. It holds its sessions at the Cathedral's Apostle's Portal every Thursday morning. At this square, the Plaça de la Mare de Déu, the central fountain is a tribute to the irrigation network.

For years, the area around Valencia has been supplying national and international markets with daily fresh produce. Now this agricultural activity is not the priority in the Valencian economy, because the industrial and services sectors (especially tourism) contribute a greater volume of revenue to the GDP. Nonetheless, the small-plot agricultural area continues to exist wherever speculation to develop and industrialise the territory has not attained the great pressure exercised on the capital's outlying neighbourhoods.

A drive along Bulevar Nord and Bulevar Sud can still reveal plots that are cultivated on a daily basis, farmsteads and farmhouses where people still work

← Cycling along the start of the Via Xurra. In the background - Cooperativa Espai Verd

Irrigation ditch between tiger nut fields

Hortolà (horticultural farmer)

↑ Preparing the land for tiger nut sowing ↓ Sant Miquel dels Reis Monastery

their horticultural fields, orchards and orange groves, irrigation channels and paths dividing up the territory in small parcels where agriculture is intensive and market farming is practiced. Farmers generally own the land and live off it, hence their interest in cultivating and harvesting several crops per year.

Orxata (tiger nut milk) from Alboraia

The small-plot agriculture surrounding Alboraia, a town just north of Valencia, is mainly dedicated to the *xufla* (pronounced 'shoo-flah') or *chufa*, the tiger nut (a small oval tubercle), from which a refreshing drink is made called *orxata* or *horchata*. Its name comes from the Italian meaning barley water. At first it may have been somewhat darker in colour and associated with drinks made from barley and almonds. However, the traditional Valencian drink is made entirely from tiger nuts, water and sugar and, despite its milky look, contains no milk. It's commonly accompanied by *fartons* (sweet buns) at *orxateries* or *horchaterías*, i.e. tiger nut parlours, dedicated exclusively to serving *orxata*, *orxata granissada* (*orxata* with shaved ice), and *llet gelada*, a variant of *leche merengada* (sugared milk flavoured with cinnamon and lemon rind).

Monastery of Sant Miquel dels Reis

This Hieronymite monastery was built in the 16th century where a 14th-century Cistercian monastery once stood. The splendid architectural complex, surrounded by horticultural fields in the neighbourhood of Orriols, District of Rascanya, in the city's northern sector, houses the Valencian Library (Biblioteca Valenciana). It was commissioned by Germana de Foix, widow of Ferdinand the Catholic, and her third husband Ferdinand of Aragon, Duke of Calabria and Viceroy of Valencia from 1526 to 1550, so that their remains could be interred there. It is considered a precedent to El Escorial and was built by the Renaissance architects Alonso de Covarrubias and Juan de Vidaña.

Tiger nuts (*xufes/chufas*)

A variety of beans are grown in the Valencian Horta

Festivities, Traditions and Gastronomy

A falla ablaze on the *Nit de la cremà* (Burning Night)

Festivities, Traditions and Gastronomy

The beginning of spring and end of summer are the times of year with the greatest concentration of feast days and festivals in Valencian towns. The Falles tradition has become a sort of unofficial Festa Major of Valencia, eclipsing the centuries-old Corpus procession festivities as the landmark date on the annual festivities calendar, as well as overshadowing the Patron Saint festivities in May, as the Falles programme now also includes events relating to the worship of Our Lady of the Abandoned (Mare de Déu dels Desemparats). Each festivity has its typical gastronomy, though the popularity of the paella makes it an essential dish at any of the city's festivities.

Festivities, Traditions and Gastronomy

Falles

Travelling to Valencia in March, at the threshold of spring, is justified by the attraction of the traditional festivities of the Falles, dedicated to Saint Joseph (19 March). Beginning on 1 March, and particularly from 16 to 19 March, the streets are alive with demonstrations of gunpowder, fireworks, art and music, festive expressions that accompany the hundreds of wood and papier-mâché figures or *ninots* in the streets. The scenes of various *ninots* comprising a *falla* ridicule or criticise aspects of Valencian life, current affairs and habits in general. Each *falla* has its neighbourhood committee that has been holding meetings all year long at the local *casal* (civic centre) to organise the creation of their *falla* and raise funds. The largest *falles* are made in Valencia, but there are also falles celebrations in towns outside the capital.

Flower offering
The *fallers* (participants), dressed in traditional finery, walk in procession, bringing flowers to Our Lady of the Abandoned. These flowers are placed on an enormous structure to create a patterned 'dress' for the statue of the Virgin.

Mascletà
At 2 pm, thousands of people crowd together in City Hall Square for the *mascletà*, a major smoke, flash and thunder display. For ten minutes, the gunpowder goes off relentlessly, an earful of loud bangs and smoke shooting up and billowing out. The Night of Fire is a fireworks display during the Falles.

Museu Faller (Falles Museum)
This museum was created to exhibit the few *ninots* saved from being burned, called the *ninots indultats* (pardoned figures), in contrast to all the other *ninot* creations, which are burned on the night of the 19th. The best *ninot* is chosen by popular vote and 'pardoned'.

Corpus Christi

Since medieval times and until recently, it was the city's biggest festival, in which the artisan guilds and different sectors of the population would participate in a procession, accompanied by decorated carriages or floats, people representing Biblical episodes and representatives of the parishes. The calendar date varies (sometime in May or June), since it falls on the first Sunday after the Pentecostal octave or eight days of Pentecost, which is itself a moveable feast.

The festival programme consists of various episodes taking place in some of the nicest streets of the Old City. It begins with the Cavalcada del Convit (opening or "invitational" parade), including the dwarves and giants and a variety of dances (ribbon, garland, stick and hobby horse dances, among others). Buckets of water are also dumped onto the organising troupe from the balconies as it passes.

In the afternoon, there is a procession with 'triumphal carriages', or religious floats called Roques, pulled by teams of horses. And finally, the large monstrance is paraded through the streets, accompanied by the faithful from the historical parishes.

La Custòdia (The Monstrance)

This processional monstrance (*custòdia*) is one of the most beautiful (and the largest) in Spain. Its silver ornamentation weighs 600 kg and the gold details weigh 8 kg. As it passes through La Seu and El Mercat neighbourhoods, rose petals are showered on it from the many balconies along the way.

Les Roques

The *Roques* (literally 'rocks') are former mystery play pageant wagons first used in processions in 1373. Two evenings before Corpus, they are rolled out to Our Lady Square by the festival's enthusiasts so they can be admired by the public.

The Dance of la Moma

La Moma is a figure representing virtue, surrounded by the seven deadly sins, with whom she carries out various dances. Under the female attire is a man, concealed by a mask and generally wearing white.

All year round

In Valencia, there are festivals for all tastes and beliefs. The calendar of festivities honours tradition with strings of bangers and fireworks displays, marching bands and regional dances. Industrialisation has not stopped the festivals from continuing to showcase an artisanal world associated with artistic creation. Let's take a look at some of them. Every 9 October, James I of Aragon's conquest of Valencia from the Moors in 1238 is commemorated. This is the Valencian Community's National Day, because it represents the creation of its self-government. Holy Week is only celebrated in the Poblats Marítims district along the coast, the two most notable events being the Procession of the Holy Interment and the Parade of Glory. On 23 June, the shortest night of the year is celebrated with a ritual of jumping over the waves seven times to see wishes fulfilled, then picnicking around a bonfire. And finally, on the second Sunday of May, the statue of the Virgin of the Abandoned is transported from the basilica consecrated to her to the cathedral, followed by a procession through the Old City. She has been the patron saint of the city since 1885.

Our Lady of the Abandoned in a rose petal shower

The Valencian Land's heraldic timbre atop the senyera (flag) on 9 October

Festivities, Traditions and Gastronomy

Festivities in other towns of the Province of Valencia

In general, the annual calendar of festivities in the areas around Valencia is different to the capital. The 'Moors and Christians' (Moros i Cristians) celebrations in Ontinyent, Bocairent and Albaida evoke the border conflicts between these two parties over the course of centuries. Some of the highlights of these festivals are the luxurious costumes, the grand entrances (*entrades*) of the music bands and the two parties at war, and the celebration of the 'embassies' (*ambaixades* or *ambaixaes*), i.e. the speeches of the ambassadors for both sides made in an attempt to avert battle. La Muixeranga is a series of dances and human towers carried out in Algemesí on 7 and 8 September. The *tonada* or traditional song played on the oboe-like *dolçaina* and the *tabalet* (small drum) is very popular. La Cordà de Paterna takes place after midnight on the last Sunday of August. Specialists ignite over 2,000 *borratxos* ('drunk rockets') per minute. The celebration of the Bonfires of Saint Anthony (Fogueres de Sant Antoni Abat) in mid-January sparks a cycle of fire-oriented celebrations. The structure for the bonfire of Canals is the highest, standing 20 metres tall. And finally, there is the Tomatina of Buñol. On the last Wednesday of August, lorries bring tonnes of ripe tomatoes into the town's central square, to be thrown at one another by thousands of participants dressed in white in an epic food battle.

Moros i Cristians (Moors and Christians Festivity)

La Muixeranga

La Tomatina

Gastronomy

Valencians eat the fresh produce from the surrounding gardens harvested over the course of the seasons, as well as a great variety of fish and seafood brought in from the sea. They also eat meat from farm animals and the rice cultivated in L'Albufera. As a complement, the citrus groves and vineyards as well as varied fruit orchards allow for a gastronomy with a diversity of flavours. The innumerable types of rice dishes cooked here make this grain the staple ingredient of Valencian culinary culture. The traditional paella is cooked over a wood fire. Along with seasonal vegetables, it often contains chicken and rabbit, and sometimes even snails. Some areas tend to add peppers, beans and pork chops. Paella is an obliging dish and does well with almost any ingredients.

Valencian gastronomy and cuisine
ISBN: 978-84-8478-589-7

Esgarrat

A starter made of charcoal-grilled red peppers cut in strips, finely sliced garlic and shredded 'English-style' codfish fillet. It is usually served with a side of toast. The peppers used here, as in most other Valencian (and Spanish) recipes, are sweet, i.e. mild, not pungent, hot or spicy.

Bajoques farcides (stuffed peppers)

These red peppers are filled with rice cooked with tomato, garlic, tuna fish, flat green beans, cinnamon and saffron. They are baked for an hour and a half, then allowed to stand for 30 minutes.

Fideuà (noodle paella)

Tradition has it that some fishermen decided to make paella while out at sea. They didn't have any rice so they used vermicelli-like noodles (*fideus*) instead. It is cooked with prawns, Norway lobsters, cuttlefish, anglerfish, squid and small fish (*morralla*).

Festivities, Traditions and Gastronomy 125

Paella valenciana (Valencian paella)
The most typical Valencian paella contains chicken and rabbit, flat green beans, finely diced tomato, tender lima beans known as *garrofons*, white beans (*mongetes*) and saffron. The rice is added last, and the paella is then allowed to simmer for about 13 minutes.

Arròs al forn (oven-baked rice)
Apart from the rice, chickpeas and sliced potatoes are the main ingredients in this dish. Pork ribs and bacon are added and everything is cooked in an earthenware casserole. The rice, blood sausage and head of garlic are added last.

Arròs negre (black rice)
Typical of fishing folk, this paella-like dish is cooked with prawns, cuttlefish and small fish (*morralla*). The cuttlefish ink dyes the dish black. It usually achieves a slightly creamy consistency, and is served with *allioli* (a garlic and olive oil emulsion).

Arnadí (squash and sweet potato pudding)
A dessert of Moorish origin, it consists of baked purée of squash with sugar, almonds and pine nuts. Puréed sweet potato can also be added. In some towns, it is eaten during Holy Week.

And also...

Beyond the capital, tourist routes through the province reveal beautiful artistic heritage associated with spiritual centres, Moorish fortifications, artisan traditions, the Roman presence and a deeply-rooted musical tradition. The Valencian hegemony in the Mediterranean during the 15th century also left significant traces. By the same token, the landscape has great heritage value, especially the citrus groves and rice paddies.

Manises Ceramics

Manises and Paterna have been renowned centres of ceramics production. Manises transformed the Moorish tradition, applying gold highlights and patterns of blue on white. Paterna worked with greens and shades of burgundy or maroon.

Monasteries

The large number of monasteries dotting the region, such as La Valldigna, El Puig, Portaceli, Sant Jeroni de Cotalba, Llutxent and La Murta, reveals their cultural influence. They are located in areas of great natural beauty.

Moorish ramparts

Although the most well-preserved Moorish city walls are in Alzira's Old City, other fortifications built over the seven centuries of Moorish occupation remain in the foundations of many castles and temples.

And also... 127

Marching Bands
These bands are a deeply entrenched tradition in the festivals of the Valencian Land. Children and youth learn to play musical instruments in classes run by local associations. The two most renowned are based in the town of Llíria.

Sagunt
Cradle of Romanisation, Sagunt has a castle on a hill on the Via Augusta, the Roman Road leading roughly north-south along the Mediterranean coast of Hispania. The Roman amphitheatre has been rebuilt on the hillside and hosts a summer festival.

The Ducal Palace in Gandia
This palatial mansion in the centre of Gandia was built next to the river and is open to visitors. It still has a Gothic inner ward or courtyard (*pati d'armes*) and a 'Golden Hall' from the 17th century. It belonged to Saint Francis Borgia (Francesc de Borja).

Carcaixent
In 1781 in this city of La Ribera area, the first commercial orange grove was planted. The city offers a guided tour to the Magatzem de la Ribera, a large turn-of-the-century warehouse also known as the 'Cathedral of the Orange', the modern Agriculture Station, Navarro Daràs Park and orange groves in the area.

Published by
© Triangle Postals, 2017

Text
© Jaime Millás

Photographs
© **Joan Colomer**, flap, p. 12a, 13a, 17a, 18ab, 19b, 21ac, 24ab, 25a, 26abc, 27c, 30b, 31ab, 34, 35a, 36, 37a, 38c, 44b, 45ab, 49ab, 51b, 53a, 54bc, 55ac, 57abcd, 62d, 66a, 80ab, 81ab, 92ab, 93ab, 94a, 95, 99, 102a, 103c, 105, 110a, 111ab, 112, 113a, 114b, 126abc, 127b, 129ac © **Hans Hansen**, p. 2, 7, 11a, 13b, 14b, 16a, 22, 23abc, 24c, 32ab, 38a, 42ab, 43ab, 45c, 50, 52, 54a, 55b, 56bc, 64, 65b, 67abc, 68ab, 69abc, 70, 74b, 75abc, 89b, 90, 93c, 98b, 120, 121abc, 127a, 140b, flap © **Rafa Pérez**, p. 5, 10, 15c, 17b, 19ac, 20ab, 25b, 27a, 29c, 30a, 35b, 38b, 44a, 45d, 48, 51c, 56a, 58, 61b, 62abc, 72a, 77a, 78b, 84b, 85a, 86a, 87ab, 88ab, 94b, 96b, 97c, 102b, 103b, 113b, 114a, 118, 119c, 127c, 140ac © **Ricard Pla**, p. 6, 12b, 15b, 16b, 21b, 28ab, 29ab, 33ab, 37b, 41a, 47abc, 53c, 60, 65a, 78a, 79, 96a, 98a, 103a, 106 © **Biel Puig**, cover, p. 15a, 27b, 39abc, 40ab, 73a, 76, 77b, 82, 84a, 86b, 129b © **Oriol Aleu**, p. 108, 109a, 115ab, 124abc, 125abcd, 127d © **Laia Moreno**, p. 14a, 33c, 41b, 46, 61a, 66b, 73b, 97b, 104a, 119ab © **Pere Vivas**, p. 4, 63a, 63b, 89a © **Lucas Vallecillos**, p. 11b, 51a, 74a, 116 © **Església de Sant Nicolau de Bari i Sant Pere Màrtir**, p. 22, 23abc © **Agència Valenciana del Turisme**, p. 122b, 123abc © **Joan M. Linares**, p. 53b, 110b © **Feria Valencia**, p. 104b © **Javier Yaya**, p. 85b © **Kai Fosterling**, p. 97a © **Mateo Gamón**, p. 72b © **Palacio de Congresos de Valencia**, p. 100 © **Sebastià Torrents**, p. 109b © **Turismo Valencia**, p. 122a

Art director
Ricard Pla

Design
Joan Colomer

Translation
Catalina Girona

Printed by
Tallers gràfics Soler

Legal deposit
Me 356-2017

ISBN
978-84-8478-765-5

Printed in Barcelona

TRIANGLE POSTALS, SL
Sant Lluís
Menorca
Tel. +34 971 15 04 51
Fax +34 971 15 18 36
www.triangle.com

No part of this book may be reproduced or used in any form or by any means —including reprography or information storage and retrieval systems—without written permission of the copyright owners.

Acknowledgements
Agència Valenciana del Turisme
Bolsa de Valencia
Catedral de València
Centre Cultural de Beneficència
Circuit de la Comunitat Valenciana Ricardo Tormo
Col·legi d'Art Major de la Seda
Feria Valencia
IVAM
Museu d'Història de València
Museu de Belles Arts de València
Oceanogràfic València
Església de Sant Nicolau de Bari i Sant Pere Màrtir
Palacio de Congresos de Valencia
Pouet de Sant Vicent Ferrer
Universitat de València – Jardí Botànic
Turismo Valencia
Hotel Venecia

TRIANGLE ▾ BOOKS   www.triangle.cat

Annex Thematic Routes
Valencia

In Valencia, visitors can stroll through the streets in search of the biographical footprints of a painter, writer or musician. Those wishing to contemplate on site the beauty and majesty of a monument with a legend behind it or associated with the creation of a myth can do so as well. It is a city also catering to those seeking to visit movie or television series filming locations or the settings of a novel in person. To attend to these and other preferences and interests, travellers can draw up simple or more involved routes, establishing their itineraries according to their timetables and the effort they wish to exert.

Valencia

Sorolla and Blasco Ibáñez Route

The biography of **Joaquim Sorolla** can be discovered through the plaque on his birth home (Carrer Mantes 8) in El Mercat neighbourhood, and at Saint Martin's Church in the Sant Francesc area, where he married Clotilde, the daughter of a photographer. At the Carme Monastery, he learned to paint. His works are exhibited at the Fine Arts Museum. The monument to Sorolla at Plaça de l'Armada Espanyola evokes his beach paintings.

Author **Vicente Blasco Ibáñez** also had creations associated with the sea when he wrote from his chalet in La Malva-rosa, now a museum. In Carrer Editor Manuel Aguilar is a plaque documenting his place of birth. A sculpture by Nassio Bayarri pays tribute to him in El Mercat neighbourhood, a popular area often appearing in his novels.

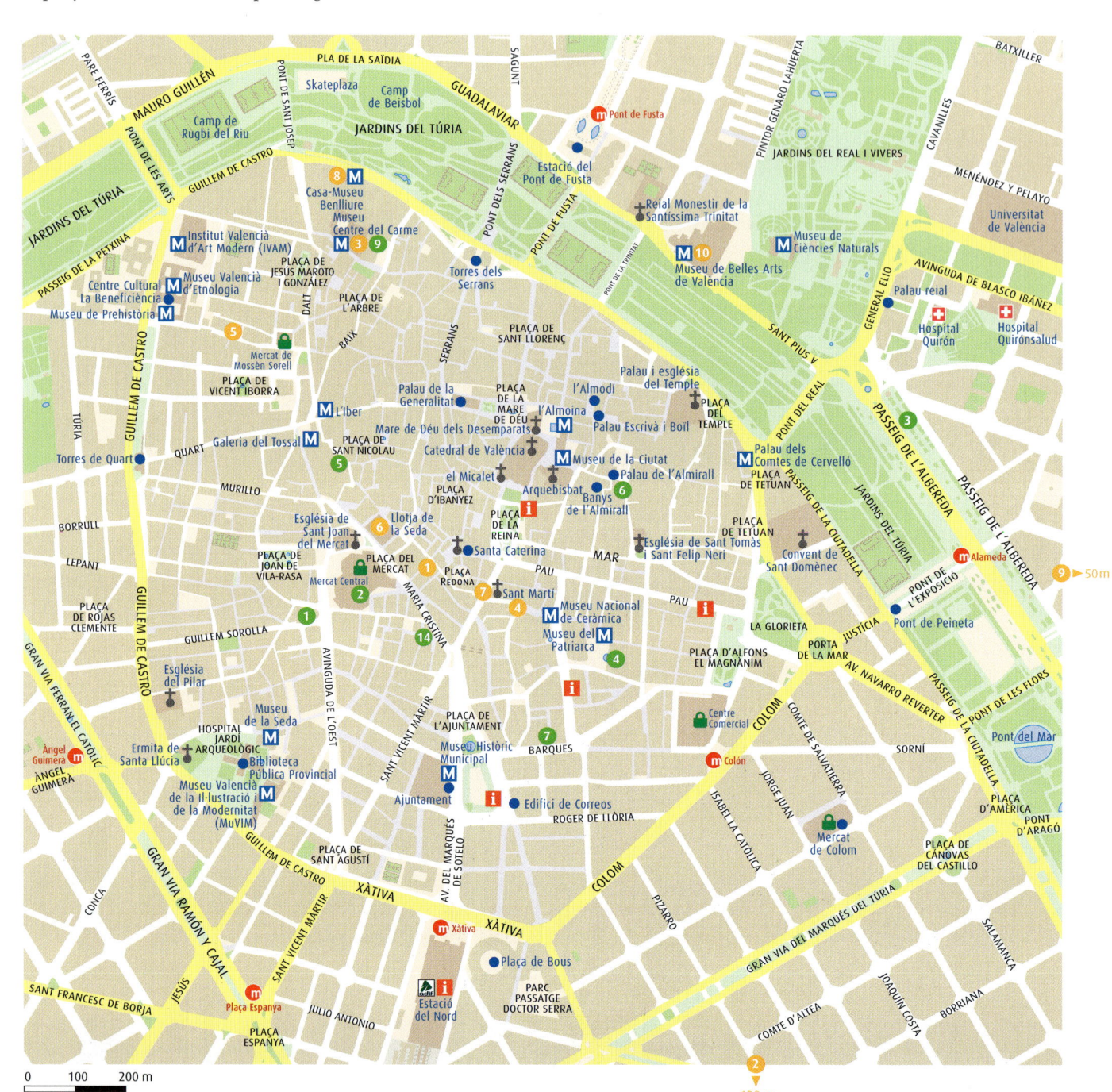

Annex Thematic Routes

🟡 Sorolla Route

1 Birth home (Carrer de les Mantes) **2** Former Escola d'Artesans (decorative arts school) **3** Centre del Carme **4** First studio **5** Second studio **6** Steps of the Silk Exchange **7** Saint Martin's Church **8** Benlliure House Museum **9** Palau de l'Exposició **10** Fine Arts Museum **11** Malva-rosa Beach **12** Casa del Bous **13** Valencia's Monument to Sorolla **14** Painting collection at the Lladró Museum (in Tavernes Blanques).

🟢 Blasco Ibáñez Route

1 Birth home (c/ Editor Manuel Aguilar) **2** Mercat Central **3** L'Albereda **4** La Nau **5** Plaça del Forn de Sant Nicolau **6** Lo Rat Penat **7** Teatre Principal **8** Vicente Blasco Ibáñez House Museum **9** Centre del Carme **10** El Cabanyal **11** Malva-rosa Beach **12** L'Horta de València (market garden area) **13** L'Albufera **14** Plaça Porxets **15** Biblioteca Valenciana (library, Sant Miquel dels Reis Monastery).

Valencia

Modernisme Route

There are five focal points of Modernisme architecture, the Valencian equivalent of Art Nouveau, in the city. The first is the Eixample or Expansion District and Columbus Market. Estació del Nord (North Station), Plaça de l'Ajuntament (City Council Square) and Carrer de la Pau is the second area where you can enjoy the work of these architects. The third area is Mercat Central and its surroundings. On the other side of the river is the fourth Modernista area: the buildings of the 1909 Regional and 1910 National Expositions. And finally, the Poblats Marítims district showcases the popular version of Modernisme in its homes and the port's *Tinglados* or warehouses.

Eixample **1** Casa Sancho (Gran Via Marquès del Túria 1) **2** Casa Ortega (Gran Via Marquès del Túria 9) **3** Casa Noguera II (Gregori Mayans 3) **4** Mercat de Colom (Jorge Juan 19) **5** Edifici Bernardo Gómez (Jorge Juan 9) **6** Casa dels Dracs (Jorge Juan 1-3) **7** Casa Cortina (Sorní 23) **8** Casa Tatay (Gran Via Marquès del Túria 63) **9** Casa Barona (Gran Via Marquès del Túria 70) **10** Casa Chapa

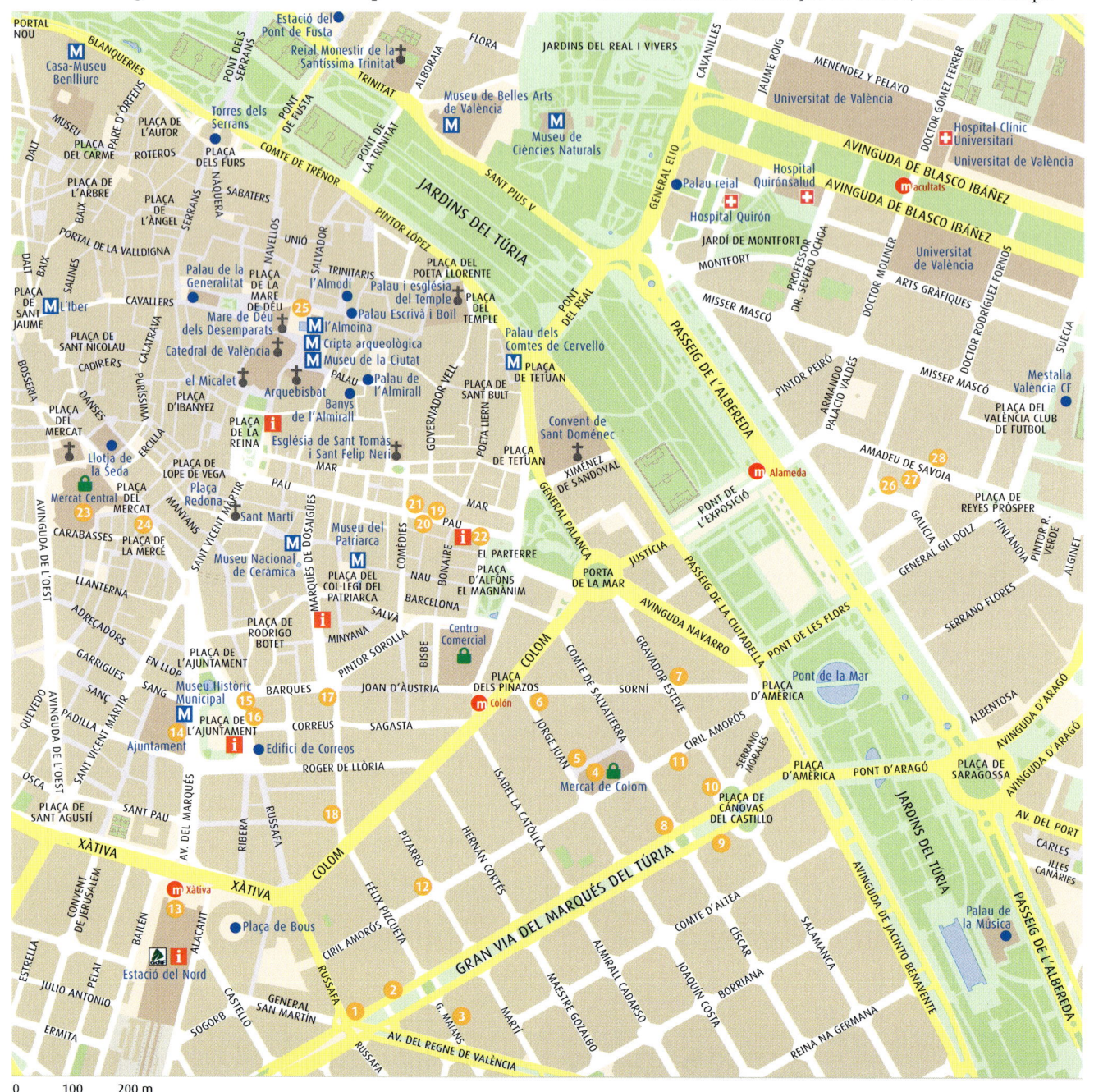

Annex Thematic Routes

(Gran Via Marquès del Túria 71) **11** Casa Peris (Ciril Amorós 74) **12** Casa Ferrer (Ciril Amorós 29).
North Station - Plaça de l'Ajuntament - Carrer de la Pau
13 Estació del Nord (Xàtiva 24) **14** City Hall façade **15** Casa Noguera I (Plaça de l'Ajuntament 22) **16** Casa Suay (Plaça de l'Ajuntament 23) **17** Banco de la Exportación (Pascual i Genís 2) **18** Edifici Niederleitner (Pascual i Genís 22) **19** Casa Grau (Pau 36) **20** Casa Sagnier (Pau 31) **21** Residential building (Pau 21-23) **22** Residential building (Pau 46).
Central Market - La Seu 23 Mercat Central **24** Casa Ordeig (Plaça del Mercat 3) **25** Casa del Punt de Ganxo (Plaça de l'Almoina 4).
Exposition Palace 26 Palau de l'Exposició Regional Valenciana de 1909 (Galícia 1) **27** Balneari de l'Alameda (Amadeu de Savoia 14) **28** Palau de la Indústria (Amadeu de Savoia 13).
Poblats Marítims District 29 Tinglados warehouses **30** Varador boathouse **31** Docks Comercials building **32** Hospital Valencia al Mar (Riu Tajo 1) **33** Examples of popular Modernisme in El Cabanyal (Reina 61, 80, 164, 173) (Barraca 198, 252) (Lluís Navarro 219, 249, 305, 309) (Progrés 262, 279) (Josep Benlliure 275, 316, 313-329) (Eduard Escalante 225, 244, 263, 265).

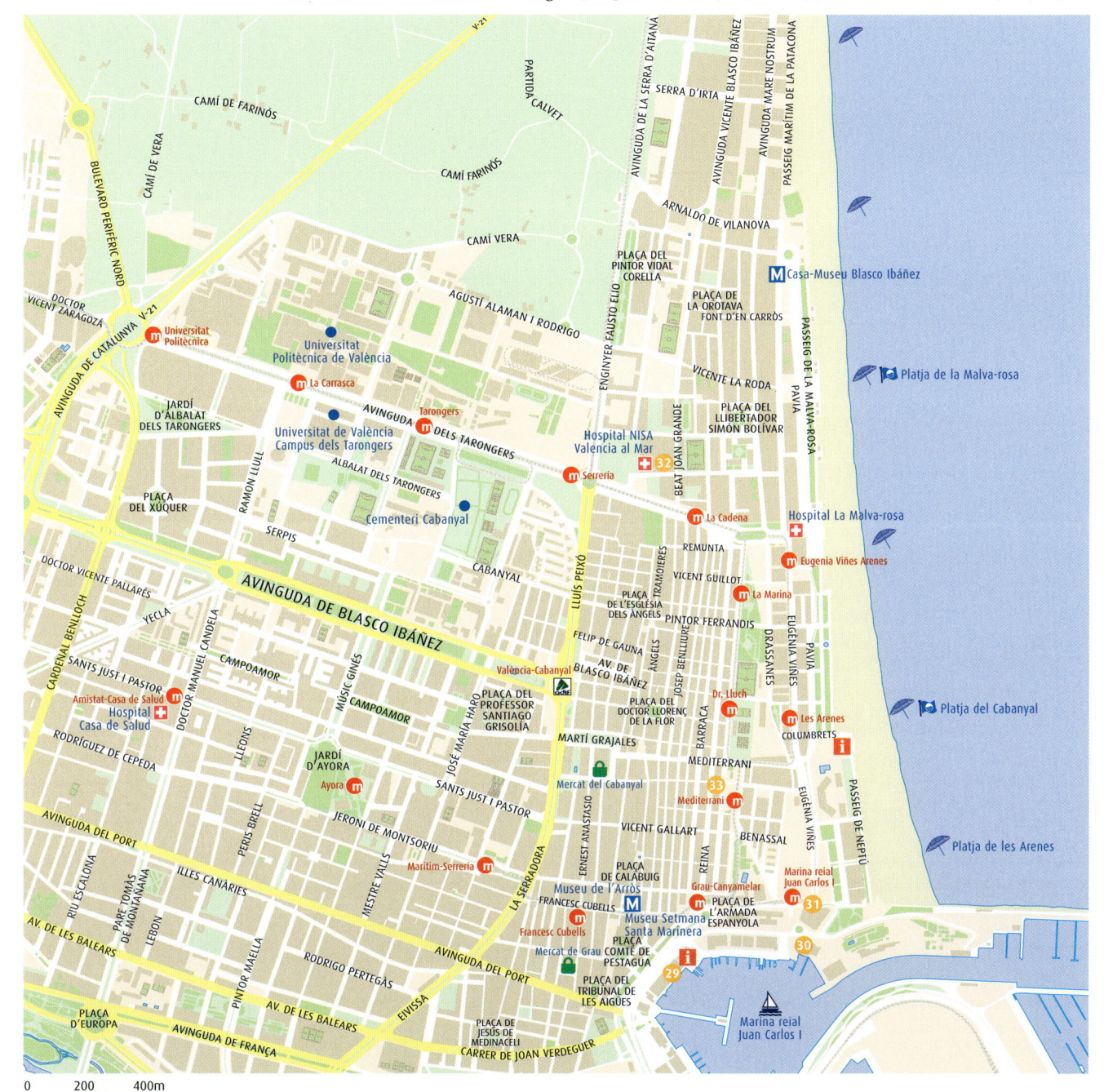

Valencia

The Old City on foot

In little over an hour's walk, you can see the most significant sights of the Old City, which was enclosed by ramparts until the late 19th century. From the Serrans Towers to the Quart Towers, as well as the Generalitat Regional Government building, the Corts Valencianes (Parliament), Ajuntament (City Hall), Diputació (Provincial Council), not to mention the main Gothic buildings, vestiges of the city's Roman and Moorish past, and its lively Modernista market hall.

1 Torres dels Serrans **2** Palau de Benicarló. Corts Valencianes **3** Palau de la Batlia. Diputació **4** Palau del Marqués de la Scala **5** Palau de la Generalitat **6** Basílica Mare de Déu dels Desemparats **7** La Seu (cathedral) **8** Plaça de la Reina **9** L'Almoina **10** L'Almodí **11** Palau del Marqués de Dosaigües **12** Palau dels Boïl d'Arenós **13** City Hall **14** Llotja de la Seda **15** Mercat Central **16** Torres de Quart

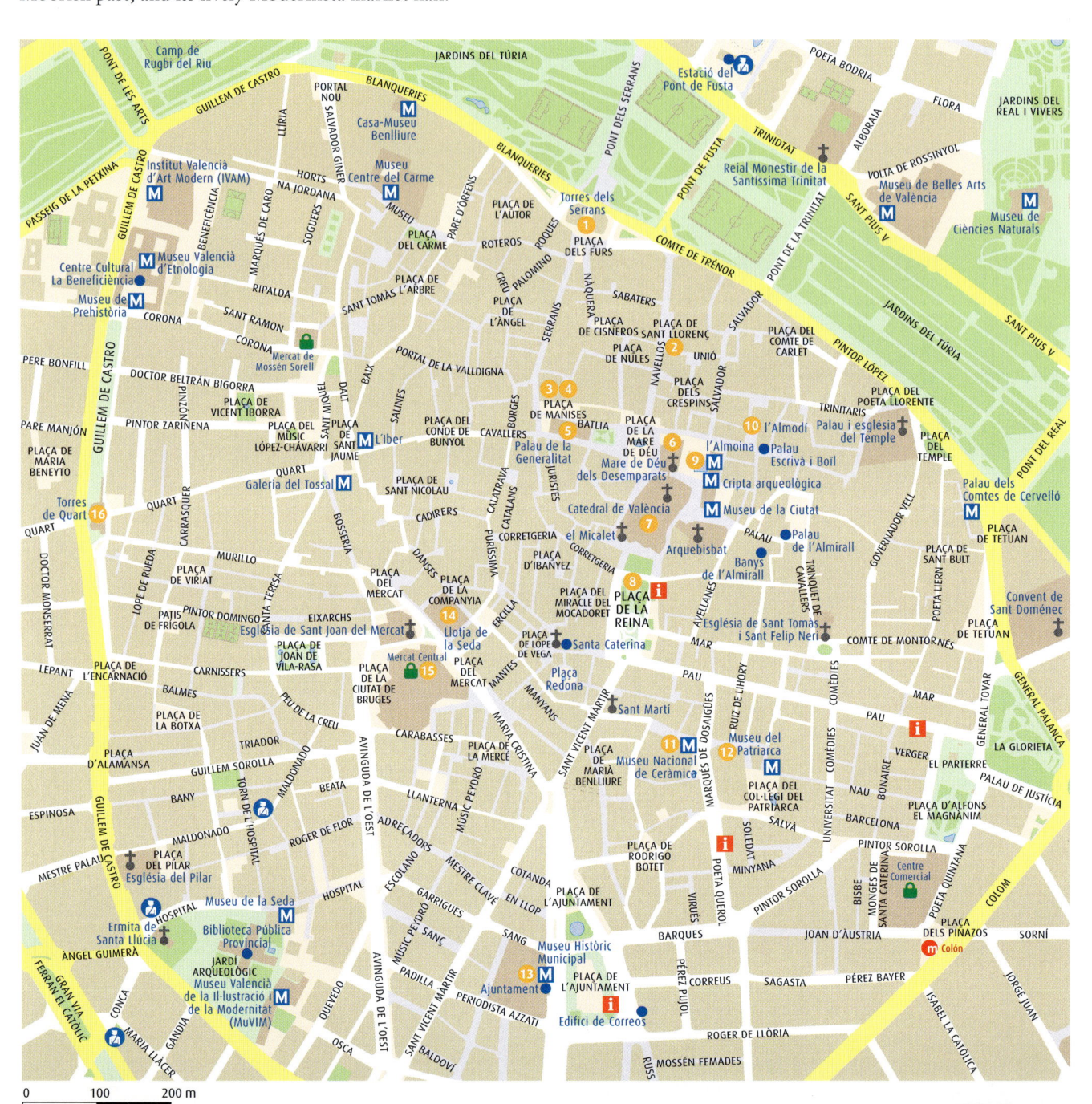

Silk Route

The College of High Silk Art allows you to discover the importance of the silk industry. It was a priority economic activity in the city until the end of the 19th century. Next to it, the Patagonia Bookshop documents that Valencia is the European capital of the UNESCO International Silk Road Project until 2020, at 9,090 km from Xi'an, where it begins. It was in the Velluters or Velvet-Makers' neighbourhood where the silk manufacturing workshops were located. At the Llotja de la Seda, commercial transactions were carried out.

Falles Route: Valencia during the Falles

During the Falles Festival, the streets are filled with women wearing magnificent traditional silk outfits. At the offering of flowers to the city's patron saint, thousands of *falleres* sport silk in a myriad of colours and patterns. The *falles* receiving the most significant artistic awards are a must. During the *mascletà*, the Falles Queen and her cortège gather on the Town Hall balcony. To see the sculptures that are 'pardoned' or saved from the flames, visit the Falles Museum.

1 College of High Silk Art **2** Patagonia Bookshop **3** Llotja de la Seda **4** Plaça de la Mare de Déu | *Falles:* **5** Plaça de l'Ajuntament **6** Na Jordana (Portal Nou) **7** Convent de Jerusalem **8** Plaça del Pilar **9** Cuba **10** Sueca-Literat Azorín **11** Regne de València-Duc de Calàbria **12** Almirall Cadarso-Comte d'Altea | **13** Falles Museum.

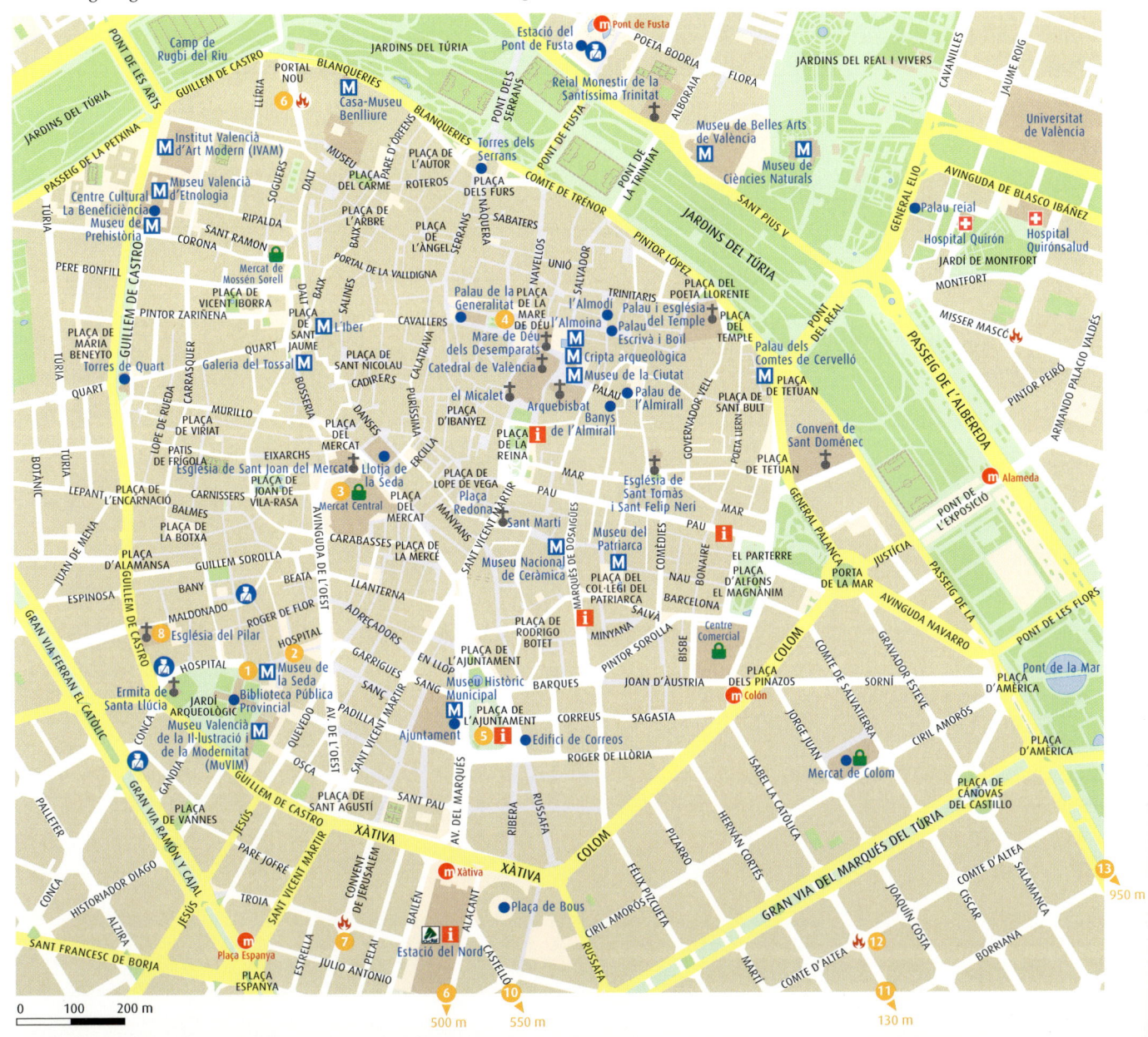

Valencia

Valencia by bicycle

Because Valencia is a flat city with very little rain and a balmy average temperature, cycling is ideal for tranquilly exploring the city's atmosphere. The distances in the historic centre are not particularly long. Itineraries from the centre to the port and city beaches are also comfortable and easy.

Valenbisi is a city bicycle service allowing you to take a bike at your starting point and park it at a Valenbisi station at your destination once you've purchased a short-term card.

There are also many bicycle hire shops in tourist areas such as the historic centre and along the Túria riverbed. A 5-kilometre cycling ring allows you to cycle along the perimeter of the former city walls, following the same route as Bus 5-Interior. This allows you to get an overview of the most traditional neighbourhoods. From this ring path, seven routes connect the centre with the university campuses, the port, the north and south beaches and other interesting destinations.

Annex Thematic Routes

The route along the Túria Gardens is the most tranquil, as it is free of all automobile traffic.

Another cycling route for travellers with a love of sports is the 24-km return trip to the Natural Park of L'Albufera, which takes you on a coastal path along the beaches.

Valencia Cycling Route

1 Túria Gardens **2** Serrans Towers **3** Plaça de Manises **4** Plaça de la Mare de Déu **5** Cathedral and Micalet **6** Plaça de l'Almoina **7** Palace of the Marquis of Dosaigües **8** Former University of Valencia building **9** El Patriarca **10** Pont de l'Exposició **11** Former Tobacco Factory **12** Palace of the Exposition **13** Pont de les Flors **14** Palau de la Música **15** Ciutat de les Arts i les Ciències **16** Marina Real Juan Carlos I **17** Seafront Promenade.

Valencia

Routes through the Albufera area

The Natural Park of L'Albufera can be visited on foot along the dunes and by boat, which can be hired at various fisherman's jetties on the lagoon, allowing you to explore the lake and observe its wealth of flora and fauna. The Park Information Centre is in El Palmar, in the Racó de l'Olla area, along with an observation tower from which to view migrating birds nesting in the reed beds of Mata del Fang.

L'Albufera on foot

There are various starting points for the marked itineraries. Please abide by park rules and regulations.

La Devesa de l'Albufera: 1 Botanical itinerary **2** Itinerary of the senses **3** El Saler historic itinerary **4** Pujol historic itinerary **5** Leisure itinerary along the beach **6** Landscape itinerary | **L'Albufera de València Natural Park: 7** and **8** Red Route: El Racó de l'Olla **9** Green Route: Na Molins **10** Blue Route: Port de Catarroja - Tancat de la Pipa.

L'Horta by bicycle: Via Xurra

The Via Xurra is a cycling greenway running along the elevated path of a former railway line. It crosses the most agricultural municipalities of Valencia's outlying Horta Nord area. The name refers to the railway line that connected the capital with Saragossa. The Aragonese and inland Valencians who speak Spanish with an Aragonese accent are called *xurros* or *churros* in Valencia.

It covers a distance of 18 km that provides no difficulty since the path is completely flat. It begins at the start of Bulevard Nord, near Avinguda de Barcelona, and ends at the railway station of Puçol. The Rafelbunyol commuter rail currently runs along the same corridor, as do the long-distance trains to Barcelona.

The path is made of compacted earth and is thus accessible to wheelchairs, except in an 800-metre section between Meliana and Albalat dels Sorells.

The route runs through Alboraia's broad expanse of tiger nut (*xufla* or *chufa*) fields, across the popular Carraixet Riverbed, and amid the orange groves and horticultural plots displaying the agricultural wealth of the greater Valencia metropolitan area.

One of the most picturesque points is the area around the former Ara Christi Charterhouse, now a social centre hosting weddings and conventions, and the hills of El Puig, where James I of Aragon prepared his conquest of Balansiya (Valencia) from the Moors.

1 Tiger nut fields of Alboraia
2 Carraixet Riverbed
3 Orange groves in La Pobla de Farnals
4 Ara Christi Charterhouse
5 El Puig hills
6 Puçol

Valencia

Tapas and Appetizers Route

In Valencia, there's an infinite number of bars sprinkled throughout the neighbourhoods, places where you can sit and have a coffee, a beer or a glass of wine with a tapa (bite to eat), sandwich delis with delicious combinations, craft or brand-name beer halls and appetizer and *montadito* tapa franchises. The most popular tapas are: griddled cuttlefish; fried squid; *esgarraet* (pepper and codfish salad); *clòtxines* (steamed Mediterranean mussels); cod balls; snails; tellina or coquina clams (delicious small bivalves); *patates braves* (fried potatos with a slightly spicy sauce). A few bars with a local following: Tasca Ángel (Carrer de l'Estamenyeria Vella 2), Bar Pilar (Carrer del Moro Zeid 13), Bar Amorós (Carrer d'en Llop 3), Taberna Vasca Ché (Avinguda Regne de València 9), Maipi (Carrer del Mestre Josep Serrano 1), Bodega Montaña (Carrer Josep Benlliure 69).

Vermut time - a vermouth & appetizer tradition

Valencia for runners

The tradition of popular road runs (the Popular Saint Sylvester Race, on 30 December), the many *voltes a peu* ('walkabouts', actually running races) organised in the different neighbourhoods over the past few years and the impulse of the Sociedad Deportiva Correcaminos club and the City Council have contributed to Valencia's becoming a European running mecca every November, when some 30,000 athletes from nearly 60 countries (above all Italy and the Netherlands) flock to the city to participate in the marathon and its 10K offshoot. Hundreds of joggers also use the open circuit through the Túria Gardens on a daily basis, as well as the routes along the boardwalk and the port, with hardly any risk of rain or cold weather.

Túria Gardens in the afternoon

Valencia with kids

The Túria Gardens offer three areas of interest for children. At the Parc de la Capçalera (Headwaters Park) is the Bioparc zoo and the opportunity to take a spin around the lake on a skateboard or scooter. In the vicinity of the Oceanogràfic (aquarium), a gigantic Gulliver lies on the former riverbed, awaiting the visit of playful kids. This sculptural playground is a large-scale reproduction (67 metres long and 9 high) of the character created by Jonathan Swift. The folds of his clothing are gigantic slides. In the aquarium complex, the dolphinarium, the belugas and the penguins are the delight of children. Another option is to take a boat ride on the Albufera lagoon. In the parks in Doctor Waksman and nearby Germans Maristes Avenues, kids can also play with the figures of Snow White and Mort & Phil (*Mortadelo y Filemón*).

Gulliver Park

TRIANGLE▼BOOKS